DIHLM

How

Th

Do you have to be a genius to get a first at university?

In *How to Get a First* Thomas Dixon argues that you do not, and sets out to demystify first-class degrees in the arts, humanities and social sciences, clearly articulating the difference between the excellent and the merely competent in undergraduate work.

This concise, no-nonsense guidebook will give prospective and current students advice on teaching and learning styles that prevail at university, and on how to manage their two most important resources – their time and their lecturers. In an accessible, and entertaining style, the author looks at subjects such as:

- making the transition from school to university
- developing transferable skills
- making use of lectures and seminars
- using libraries and the internet
- note-taking, essays, seminars and presentations
- common mistakes to avoid
- writing with clarity and style
- revision and examinations.

Illustrated with many examples from a range of academic disciplines, *How to Get a First* is an all-purpose guide to success in academic life. For more tips and useful links, visit: www.getafirst.com

Thomas Dixon has taught at the Universities of Cambridge and London and is now a Lecturer in History at Lancaster University.

How to Get a First

The essential guide to
academic success

Thomas Dixon

Routledge
Taylor & Francis Group

LONDON AND NEW YORK

First published 2004 by Routledge
2 Park Square, Milton Park, Abingdon, Oxon, OX14 4RN

Simultaneously published in the USA and Canada
by Routledge
270 Madison Avenue, New York, NY 10016

Reprinted 2005 (twice), 2006

Routledge is an imprint of the Taylor & Francis Group

© 2004 Thomas Dixon

Typeset in 10.5/12pt Bembo by Graphicraft Limited, Hong Kong
Printed and bound in Great Britain by
TJ International Ltd, Padstow, Cornwall

British Library Cataloguing in Publication Data
A catalogue record for this book is available from the
British Library

Library of Congress Cataloging in Publication Data
Dixon, Thomas (Thomas M.)
  How to get a first : the essential guide to academic success /
Thomas Dixon.
       p. cm.
  Includes bibliographical references and index.
  ISBN 0–415–31732–0 (hardback : alk. paper) —
  ISBN 0–415–31733–9 (pbk. : alk. paper)
    1. College student orientation.   2. Study skills.
  3. Report Writing.   I. Title.
  LB2343.3.D574 2004
  378.1'98—dc22

                                        2004002094

ISBN 0–415–31732–0 (hbk)
ISBN 0–415–31733–9 (pbk)

Contents

Preface   vii
Acknowledgements   ix

1 Introduction   1

2 Taking aim: the task and the resources   20

3 Lectures, classes and seminars   33

4 Libraries and reading lists   42

5 Reading and taking notes   59

6 Using the internet   74

7 Planning an essay, presentation or dissertation   85

8 Giving a presentation   94

9 Writing essays and dissertations I: the basics   104

10 Writing essays and dissertations II:
    arguing with style   125

11 Revision and exams   152

12 How to get a first   164

    Further reading   168
    Index   170

Preface

This book has arisen from my experiences both of studying and of teaching at undergraduate and postgraduate levels in a range of academic disciplines (history, philosophy, religious studies and theology), primarily at the Universities of Cambridge and London. In effect, it is what I wish I had known prior to starting my university career. I hope it will help equip others to make the most of their potential and get the most out of their degree. The title of the book, *How to Get a First*, will make most sense to students in universities where final degree results are divided, as they are in Britain, into the classes of 'first', 'two-one' or 'upper second', 'two-two' or 'lower second', and 'third'. The advice this book offers on academic success will, of course, also apply just as much to students at institutions where this classing system does not operate.

Acknowledgements

I am grateful to the staff and students of the following institutions for the opportunities they have afforded me to teach, to learn, and to think about academic skills. At Cambridge University: the Faculty of Divinity, the Department of History and Philosophy of Science, King's College, and Churchill College; at London University: the London Centre for the History of Science, Technology and Medicine, Imperial College, University College, and Birkbeck College. Several individuals have particularly encouraged me to think about academic skills and to write this book. One of my undergraduate supervisors at King's College, Cambridge, Nick Adams, was the first person to get me to think about academic writing as a skill and about what constituted excellent academic work. More recently, Emma Dixon, Gordon Dixon, Kay Dixon, Miri Freud-Kandell, Monica Gonzalez, James Humphreys, Chris Insole, Tim Jenkins, Diana Lipton, Peter Lipton, Rebecca Nye, Lewis Owens, Rosalind Paul, Greg Radick, Rebecca Stott, Denys Turner, Léon Turner, Fraser Watts, and Anna Williams have all offered very helpful ideas and encouragement in connection with this book. Two anonymous readers for Routledge made invaluable suggestions about how to improve it. Michael, Jackie, Patrick and Alex Dixon encouraged me to think about the differences between teaching and learning at school and at university. Anna Clarkson, Jessica Simmons, Philip Mudd, Priyanka Pathak, Geeta Rampal, Hannah Qualtrough and Jon Raeside at RoutledgeFalmer have all dealt with the various stages of production of this book extremely efficiently; I am very grateful to them for all their help, and to Sue Hadden for her meticulous management of the copyediting and proofreading process. Many thanks to Trevor

Sather at SquareEye.com for his excellent work on the companion website. Finally, I particularly want to thank Emily Butterworth for her endless encouragement and advice while I was working on the final version of this book.

Chapter 1

Introduction

Summary

Read this book before you get to university! Be prepared for the differences between teaching and learning at university and at school. You don't have to be a genius to get a first in your university degree. You do need to understand the tasks, acquire the right skills and spend plenty of time practising them. If you can learn to read actively and selectively, think clearly and creatively, and to speak and write in plain English, you will be able to excel at university.

One in 10

Roughly speaking, out of every 10 students who graduate from a UK university each year, only one comes out with a first-class degree. About five get an upper second, three a lower second, and the remaining one gets either a third-class or an unclassified degree.[1] *How to Get a First* is about how to maximise your chances of being in the top 10 per cent, rather than in the middle 80 per cent or the bottom 10 per cent. It is about the difference between competent academic work and excellent academic work.

---

1 Higher Education Statistics Agency figures for 2001–2: <http://www.hesa.ac.uk> (accessed 4 January 2004).

Who is this book for?

This book is for prospective and current undergraduate students working towards a degree in any subject in which attending lectures and seminars, giving presentations, reading books and articles, doing research in libraries and on the internet, writing assessed written work and taking examinations are key components. I expect those who will find this book most useful will be students working towards degrees in the arts, humanities and social sciences, in subjects such as English literature, history, sociology, modern languages, economics, politics, American studies, anthropology, archaeology, classics, geography, history of art, law, media studies, music, philosophy, psychology, religious studies and theology.

Since the advice I offer below is applicable across such a wide range of subjects, I have endeavoured, in what follows, to use examples from a suitably wide range of disciplines. Despite this endeavour, it is possible that you might still be able to discern the influence of my own particular experience teaching courses on the history and philosophy of science, and on theology and religious studies. You may also detect the influence of my special interest in British intellectual history of the eighteenth and nineteenth centuries. I mention this at the outset just in case you find yourself wondering, for example, about all the references to David Hume and Charles Darwin. I have tried to balance references to my own pet subjects with references to examples taken from a wide range of other disciplines and from other times and places.

How to Get a First contains advice relating to all the most important aspects of academic life, which will be relevant and helpful no matter what your aspirations. There is a particular emphasis, however, on how to excel at university. So, if you are hoping to get a first-class degree (or at least give it your best shot), are wondering what skills are involved and whether you have them, and want to know how best to spend the available time in order to achieve your goal, then this book is for you: it aims to demystify the first-class degree and explain how you can go about getting one, from your first day at university onwards.

The best time to read *How to Get a First* is before you even get to university. Then you will arrive at university with your eyes open and with a clear idea of the challenges ahead and how to meet them most effectively. It will also equip you to know what to expect from your lecturers and tutors. If you have had a gap year between school and university, reading this book will be a particularly helpful way to re-engage with the academic world before starting your course. Whether or not you have had a gap year, it will help to prepare you for some of the differences between the teaching and learning styles that are most prevalent at university and those with which you are familiar from school.

Finally, I also hope that this book will be helpful to secondary-school teachers who are responsible for providing guidance and advice to A-level students preparing to make the transition to university. It will perhaps provide a helpful glimpse of some of the attitudes, values and teaching styles that their students will encounter at university.

What is this book for?

This book is to help you improve your academic performance by asking yourself basic but important questions such as 'How can I get more out of my classes and lectures?', 'How could I improve my academic writing style?', 'Could I save time by reading books and articles more efficiently?' and 'How can I make sure I feel confident and prepared when I go into my exams?'. I hope this book will help you realise the following:

- You do not have to be a genius to get a first.
- What constitutes first-class academic work can be clearly specified – it is not mysterious.
- The keys to success are understanding the task and managing your resources.
- The central task is persuasion, using the tools of logical argument and relevant evidence.
- Your two most important resources are your time and your lecturers.
- The whole system is set up to help you succeed – all you need to do is co-operate.
- Thinking clearly and writing clearly are two sides of the same coin: academic writing should not be complicated, abstract or jargonistic.

I also hope that this book will serve as a sort of all-purpose companion to your academic studies. It contains thoughts and advice relating to all aspects of your work. You will probably find it helpful to read the book once straight through (which should not take long – it is an easy read), and then refer back to specific sections when the time comes in due course to focus on a particular element in the range of academic activities, such as planning an essay, giving a presentation, or revising for exams.

What is this book not?

This is not an academic book. It does not draw on educational research and theory, nor does it employ technical concepts from those areas. The writing style I adopt in this book is also, in some ways, non-academic. For instance, I make use of bullet-point lists; I use italics for extra emphasis in some places; I use chatty contractions such as 'let's' and 'don't'; and I even use exclamation marks from time to time! All of these are things that you would not normally expect to find in academic writing. I have also used many more sub-headings to divide up the text than I would have done had I been writing an academic article or book. *How to Get a First* is, then, a non-academic book about academic life; it is a concise, no-nonsense guidebook for students, offering inside information on how to deal with the academic side of university life. Do as I say, not as I do in this book!

How to become an Olympic medal-winning gymnast

If you wanted to become an Olympic medal-winning gymnast, you would have to undertake a long and intensive training programme. You would need to learn unfamiliar skills and new physical movements of which you had known nothing before. You would think it rather odd if your trainer never introduced you to these new skills, nor told you how to perform those new movements, but instead would get you to come along once a week to perform a routine of your own invention and then simply say 'No, that's no good. Do a better routine next week.' To excel at something you need to be told and shown what excellence involves, and instructed in how to go about trying to achieve it.

Too often, in the past, undergraduate students have been put in a position similar to that of the aspiring gymnast with the unhelpful coach – they were expected to excel academically at university but not given a clear picture of how to do so nor given enough guidance with respect to the new skills they needed to learn, and how these differed from what they were used to at school. This book is an attempt, based on my own experiences both as a student and, now, as a lecturer, to provide some guidance about the skills that you will need to develop in order to succeed academically. This is only a starting point. During the course of your own university career you will need to refine and polish these basic skills. There is, of course, no simple formula that can guarantee academic success, nor any set of rules which, if you read them and tried to follow them, could ensure that you would get a first. The advice and guidance contained in this book should, however, give you a good idea of what is required and help you maximise your chances of success.

Essay-writing, essay-writing, essay-writing

The training programme for your degree will probably have four main elements:

- Attending lectures, classes and seminars
- Reading books and articles
- Writing essays
- One-to-one or small-group tutorial contact with teaching staff.

The most important of these four elements is the third: writing essays.

Writing essays is difficult ...

Essay-writing is the most underrated and underdeveloped, and yet the most important of academic skills. Too many people think that to do well at university you must simply go to lectures, read books, absorb the information and then reproduce it in assessed work and exam essays. This overlooks the crucial fact that writing an essay is not a simple matter of spilling onto the page all the ideas that you have ingested; rather, it is a difficult and highly skilled craft. Writing clearly and persuasively is only possible if you think clearly and understand the material you are dealing with. Writing well and thinking well go hand in hand. To do well at university you need to do both.

The aim, which is the goal to have in mind throughout your training programme, is to be able to produce grammatically correct, elegant, concise, well-informed, clear, logical, thought-provoking and persuasive essays.

In most arts and humanities degrees, you are assessed primarily by one criterion: your ability to produce good written work. (In some cases oral presentations will contribute to your marks, and in the case of degrees with a linguistic component, translations, orals and other language exercises will contribute a significant amount.) A proportion of this work is likely to be made up of essays written under quite stressful exam conditions. In short, to excel under this system you must be an excellent writer.

... but not that difficult

At the other end of the spectrum from those who think that writing essays is effortless are those who, equally misguidedly, think that writing essays is impossible. It is good to be ambitious and quite right to have high standards, but you will not be able to produce excellent essays straight away without any practice, and you will not always be able to live up to your highest standards. Do not aim always to produce an absolutely *perfect* essay – that would be unrealistic. It is more important that you produce essays (whether they are to be formally assessed or not), of the length required by the deadline you are given. You will then receive feedback on this work, with a view to developing your skills further. For some people, the result of having their standards set too high can be that they produce no work at all – because their perfectionism will not allow them to hand in work with any flaws. It is absolutely natural and normal to write essays with imperfections, omissions and faults – even the best writers do not write *perfect* essays.

Different sorts of written work

The written work you produce in the course of your degree will fall into one or more of these four categories:

*   Essays that are not formally assessed
*   Assessed essays
*   Dissertations
*   Exam essays.

(Oral presentations rely on some of the same reading, thinking and communication skills as written work, but there are differences; see Chapter 8.) If you take a degree course which includes producing written work that is not formally assessed (that is, the mark does not count towards your final degree result), this is an excellent opportunity to develop and test your writing skills in a relatively pressure-free context. Hopefully you will then have already developed your writing skills to a high level when you come to be appraised in your exams or other assessed written work. The 'supervision' and 'tutorial' systems at Cambridge and Oxford put particular emphasis on the production of regular essays for informal assessment throughout the year.

There are differences between non-assessed essays, assessed essays, dissertations, and exam essays; and each is discussed below. Assessed pieces will be longer and, sometimes, will include a little more background and discussion than the time-pressure of an exam may allow. They should also be more polished and include accurate references and a bibliography. But, as a rule, you should approach writing academic essays – whether for informal feedback, formal assessment, or for an exam – according to the same basic principles: you are being asked to write a well-informed, logical, persuasive, and clearly structured answer to a specific question. You should get into the habit of producing well-structured, well-written essays from the outset so that you know how to do so when it comes to the most important pieces of assessed written work and exams.

From school to university

If you are reading this book before arriving at university, it will be useful to think about how academic work at degree level will be different from what you have been used to at school. Even if you have already started a degree course it still might be useful to reflect on what your experiences have revealed about the different teaching and learning styles that prevail at school and at university, and on how to cope with those differences. One of the main differences between school and university is that at university a lot of the teaching comes in the form of lectures rather than classes or seminars, which are the predominant forms at school. You will need to work out how to make the most of lectures and how to take useful notes. This is discussed in Chapter 3. What are the other fundamental differences to be prepared for?

Taking the initiative

The most obvious and important difference is that as a university student you are expected to take a lot of the initiative for yourself. It is basically down to you to find out when your lectures and classes are, where they are taking place, who your tutor is, what library and internet resources are available to you, what networks of pastoral support are in place, and so on. It is down to you to find the books and articles that your lecturers and tutors ask you to read. It is down to you to produce written work on time; your lecturers will not be standing over you making sure you get down to work, nor reminding you when the deadline is. It is also down to you to seek out your lecturer or tutor if things are not going well and to explain the problems you are having.

School teachers and university lecturers

You will also soon learn that school teachers and university lecturers are very different creatures. It might be that you loved all your school teachers and found them to be caring, supportive and reasonable. It is possible, however, that some of your teachers seemed strict or over-demanding; perhaps they seemed not to understand you – not to be on your wavelength; perhaps they seemed harsh, even sadistic; perhaps you thought they had very poor social and communication skills. Well, if so, you ain't seen nothing yet! You should be prepared to meet all of these faults on an entirely new scale when you come into contact with university lecturers. Hard though it may be to believe, on balance school teachers are a lot more accommodating, understanding, encouraging and socially skilled than university lecturers. You will find, most probably, that your lecturers are a lot more prepared than your school teachers were to dish out criticism and that they are a lot less practised at combining that criticism with encouragement, empathy and appreciation.

There is one particularly significant difference between school teachers and university lecturers, of which you should be aware from the outset. University lecturers, unlike school teachers, lead a sort of double life. They are responsible for designing and delivering undergraduate lecture courses, for setting exams and for marking assessed work. This is similar to the role of the school teacher – preparing and teaching lessons and setting and marking homework, assessed work and exams. University lecturers, however, as well as being employed to teach undergraduate and postgraduate students, are employed to pursue their own academic research. The question of how to balance teaching and research is pressing and constant for most university lecturers. As a result it is possible, although hopefully relatively rare, that you will feel that your lecturer's teaching is not getting her full attention. This could be because she is preoccupied with writing a review, article or book which is due to be submitted. Academics are judged, by current and potential employers, primarily by the quantity and quality of the publications arising from their research. This is therefore bound to be one important focus of their working lives.

I offer this description of the life of the academic simply to explain the balance that your lecturers have to achieve between teaching and research, not to defend or condone lecturers who let their teaching suffer or who let their students feel like unwelcome distractions. The relationship between teaching and research should be managed in such a way that the two feed into each other. A lecturer's own specialised research into, say, the circumstances and context of the composition of a particular philosophical tract in the seventeenth century should allow her to give her students fresh insights when giving an introductory seminar on that text, even if she cannot go into much detail in that context. And the questions and problems raised by students in such a seminar, and the obstacles she runs into when trying to explain the material to a student audience, should be instructive when it comes to writing up her research in a clear and persuasive way for an academic audience in due course. That is the ideal. It is important to understand how lecturers might succeed or fail in their attempt to attain this ideal if you are going to understand how and why lecturers and school teachers differ.

So far I have been focusing on the negative side of dealing with university lecturers, and you should certainly be prepared for the fact that you might have to deal with difficult and demanding teachers at university. However, it would be entirely unfair to give the impression that anything but a small proportion of academics are socially incompetent, other-worldly, bookish types concerned with their own minuscule area of research specialism to the exclusion of all else, including the needs of their students. This picture is a misleading caricature. The good news is that the majority of university lecturers take their teaching extremely seriously and provide stimulating lectures, classes and seminars, which provide opportunities for you to have access to someone with a very high level of knowledge, expertise and sophistication on a particular subject. Your lecturers − even those with negligible social skills, bad taste in clothes and no common sense − are invaluable sources of understanding and guidance. In many cases they may be world experts on the particular topic you are studying with them. Learn how to make use of this resource. (I will come back to some of these points in the section entitled 'Manage your teachers' in Chapter 2, pages 29–32.)

Conflicting advice

One of the more frustrating things about making the transition from school to university is the fact that your lecturers will almost certainly give you advice about study skills and academic essay-writing that directly contradicts things you were told by teachers at school. You will probably find that this is true of some of the advice I offer in this book, too. The following are some of the things you may have been told about essay-writing at school, which you might well find your lecturers at university contradicting:

- You should never use the first person when writing an essay. Instead of writing 'I think that . . .' you should use some other construction such as 'It will be shown that . . .' or 'We shall see that . . .'.
- You should not start a sentence with a conjunction such as 'and' or 'but'; nor end one with a preposition such as 'with' or 'to'.
- It is bad style to use the same word too often. Therefore you should find alternatives to 'thinks' or 'says' so as to avoid constantly repeating these words. For instance, you should learn to use 'expounds', 'proposes', 'asserts', 'insists', 'affirms', and other synonyms.
- When writing an essay, you should always give a balanced account of both sides of an argument and then offer your personal conclusion.

Indeed, in the case of all these examples, I hope your university lecturers do contradict them as I think they are all unhelpful pieces of advice. The following is the sort of advice I hope you will be getting at university (and will certainly be getting in this book) instead:

- It is fine to write in the first person, and the alternative constructions that people use are often cumbersome and awkward.
- And general rules about starting sentences with conjunctions or ending them with prepositions need not always be adhered to (see Chapter 9, pages 106 and 113).
- It is also fine to use words such as 'thinks' or 'says' quite often in academic writing; the alternative is to pepper your essay with unnatural and pompous-sounding words like 'expounds' or 'affirms'.

- When writing an essay you should show an awareness of opposing points of view, but that does not mean that you have to give them an equal amount of space in your essay. You should argue your own case and back it up with evidence. You should not offer a personal adjudication on two opposing arguments if it amounts to nothing more than an unjustified personal preference.

I will talk further about all of these things in Chapters 7, 9 and 10. For the moment, the point is simply that you should be prepared to adapt the ways you learn and write in response to expectations and standards that will differ from those you have got used to at school.

You also need to be prepared for the fact that your lecturers might disagree amongst themselves on some questions of method and writing style. This is particularly annoying. Dr Biggins might tell you not to include an overview of your argument in your introductory paragraph; the following week Professor Wiggins might absolutely insist that you do. This sort of inconsistency is probably more widespread at university level than at school level. There are two things you can do about it. First, you can simply be pragmatic and learn to tailor your writing according to who will be marking the essay. To do this you need to know who will be marking the essay – which is always a useful thing to know in any case, but not always possible. You should feel free to ask your lecturers who will be marking assessed work and exams. They may or may not be prepared to tell you. The second thing you can do about inconsistent advice among your lecturers is to raise the matter explicitly with your lecturers or your tutor. A department should not be giving you conflicting advice on such matters. They should be able either to give you some definitive guidance as to which lecturer's advice to follow or (more likely) they will be able to reassure you that either style would be perfectly acceptable in an exam or assessed essay. As I will explain further below, if you write well-informed, argumentative essays, in plain English, and backed up with evidence, you cannot go far wrong, even if a particular lecturer does not favour, for instance, your style of introduction or your use of the first person.

Opinion and evidence

Perhaps the most important difference between writing essays at school and writing essays at university (and one that I will return to several times in what follows) is that while in the case of the former the emphasis may have been on developing your own *opinion*, the emphasis in the latter should be on having your own *evidence*. In English literature you must support your interpretation of, say, *King Lear*, with illustrative quotations from the text of the play; and you must explain how your interpretation differs from that of other Shakespeare scholars. In a history essay on the causes of the American Civil War you must support your assertions with facts about the extent of slave labour at the time; the nature of political debates of the time; the reasons for war given by protagonists; more recent scholarly disagreements about these, and so on. These facts must be taken from either primary or secondary material you have read in preparation for the essay and to which you have given precise references.

This may all sound obvious. Hopefully it does. However, an alarming proportion of students still produce essays with very little in the way of evidence and examples and rather a lot in the way of sweeping generalisations and personal opinions. Again, this is something I will come back to below. The point for the moment is that you should get out of the habit – if you were ever in it – of offering personal opinions that amount to no more than unsubstantiated preferences. Lecturers like nothing less than a conclusion along the following lines: 'There are strong arguments on both sides of this debate but personally I feel that, in the end, democracy will always be the fairest form of government.' Lecturers would much rather read a conclusion more like this: 'Comparing the examples of the United States, Switzerland, Nigeria and China, I have shown that there is no single concept of "democracy" which can be applied universally; it is a concept that has been used for different rhetorical and political purposes in different times and places.' In short, feelings should be replaced with facts! Preferences should be replaced with inferences (from evidence to conclusions).

Why bother?

If you are reading this book, you probably already have some idea why you want to do as well as possible at university (or you know someone else, such as your parents, who have an idea why you *should* want to and so bought you this book!). The benefits of working rather than coasting through your degree are fairly obvious. First and foremost, it is simply much more satisfying and fulfilling to tackle the challenges with which your degree course presents you head-on and to do your best to meet them than to spend three or four years of your life trying to do as little academic work as possible. A degree, like any other major challenge, is an opportunity for personal and intellectual development, if you choose to take it. If you try to excel you will enjoy the course much more.

The idea that, at university, you can choose either to work hard at your studies or to have a good time, but not both, is a complete myth. All the people I know who achieved first-class degree results had a very good time throughout their university careers too, taking full advantage of the other aspects of university life on offer (sport, drama, journalism, politics, pubs, clubs and so on). One of the things that this book should help you to discover is that by managing your time effectively and keeping the tasks in proportion, it is possible to excel in your academic work without it taking over your life. Hopefully you will find that you enjoy the time you spend studying and writing. But even if that process is not one of unalloyed pleasure, you will certainly find that the time you spend relaxing and socialising is much more enjoyable when you have earned it by doing some work.

Finally, and most obviously of all, there is the basic financial incentive. Whatever university you are studying at, and whatever the course you are taking, you will make yourself much more attractive to potential employers by having a first-class degree. Having an excellent degree result, rather than an average one, will open countless doors for you in future employment, and will significantly increase the salary you might expect to be offered. With ever-increasing numbers of young people deciding to pursue education right through to university level, having a degree, on its own, no longer marks you out to employers as someone with an unusually high level of academic achievement or of intellectual excellence. Having a first-class degree, however, still does.

Transferable skills

Before moving on from this subject of the connection between your degree and your future employment, I should mention something that you may have heard your school teachers and others refer to, namely 'transferable skills'. In the world of higher education more and more people are interested in promoting transferable skills. They are popular with (some) academics because they provide them with an additional justification for continuing to teach courses in relatively obscure subjects with little apparent practical utility. (I should add that most academics would quite rightly reject the idea that students should only be taught information with obvious practical utility; see the section at the end of this chapter on 'Romantic geniuses and management consultants', pages 17–19.) They are popular with politicians since the idea that undergraduate students are learning transferable skills at taxpayers' expense is a lot more politically palatable than the idea that they are, at public expense, being taught information on arcane academic subjects such as the symbolism of decorations on ancient Greek pottery, the philosophical doctrines of medieval theology, the rules of Anglo-Saxon syntax and grammar, the social history of the comic-book, or the interpretation of classic novels using psychoanalytic theory. And, finally, they are popular with employers since most employers want to hire people who are intellectually able and effective, but who need not be experts in art, theology, linguistics, history, or postmodern literary theory.

So what are transferable skills? They are non-subject-specific skills that you acquire or develop in the course of your degree and then transfer with you and put to good use in your workplace after you graduate. The most important ones can be summarised under three broad headings: researching, thinking and communicating. Whether you are studying history or English, American studies or music, philosophy or sociology, you will need to develop these skills if you want to do well in your degree, and you will need to develop them to a high level if you want to get a first. They are precisely the sorts of skills that will be attractive to all sorts of potential employers: from charities to the civil service, from media firms to accountants, from management consultancies to schools and universities.

The rest of this book is all about how to develop these skills with the aim of getting a first-class degree. So, for the moment, I will simply list some of the most important transferable skills as a taster of what the rest of this book will discuss in more detail:

Researching
- Using libraries
- Using the internet
- Identifying sources of authoritative information
- Gathering information quickly and reliably…
- … while also reading rigorously and carefully
- Formulating methods of recording and organising information

Thinking
- Identifying key issues
- Identifying and challenging hidden assumptions
- Differentiating between similar but distinct arguments
- Understanding how to use evidence to support or oppose arguments
- Spotting patterns
- Lateral thinking: identifying similarities between apparently independent subjects

Communicating
- Speaking and writing in plain English
- Speaking in public with confidence and authority
- Using rhetoric to engage and persuade an audience or readership
- Using evidence to argue your case
- Defending your position in the face of criticism and opposition.

In addition to these researching, thinking and communicating skills, with which this book is primarily concerned, you will also develop other transferable skills in the course of your university career. These will include organisational skills (managing your time; balancing work with extracurricular activities), interpersonal skills (dealing with lecturers and fellow students; participating in seminars and student committees), information technology skills (improving your grasp of word-processing and other software packages; using the internet), and language skills (learning one or more foreign languages in the course of your studies, whether as part of a languages degree or for other purposes).

Inside information

Why should you trust the advice I have to offer in this book? As I have said, you might find that some of it contradicts what you yourself believe, or what your teachers at school (or university) have told you. I do not believe for a moment that my way of doing things is the only good way to approach academic study. Everyone has a different way of studying, and what I advise might not always suit you. However, one good reason to take seriously the advice I offer is that I have inside knowledge of the system, both as a student and as a lecturer. I know how the system works and how to play the academic game successfully. This book, then, contains the advice accumulated over about 10 years of studying and teaching at universities in a range of arts and humanities subjects. In effect, it is the advice I wish someone had given me before I started my university career.

I can still remember being a student (just), and some of the advice in this book is simply an account of the skills and techniques that I found most useful myself when I was taking undergraduate and postgraduate degree courses. Also, for the purposes of writing this book, I put myself back in the position of an undergraduate student. I set myself a range of essay questions on topics as various as: Stoic theories of emotion; slavery and the American Civil War; blindness and madness in Shakespeare's *King Lear*; the consequences of the French Revolution; the sociology of crime; women's suffrage in Britain; 'inference to the best explanation' in the philosophy of science; belief in God and the problem of evil; Simone de Beauvoir and the construction of gender; altruism in George Eliot's *Middlemarch*; and the interpretation of the Italian Renaissance. Then I took myself off to the library, armed with essay titles, reading lists and my laptop. There I hunted for the books and articles I needed and made notes from them as quickly and accurately as possible. I used databases in the library to hunt for relevant material and trawled the internet for helpful websites. It was just like being a student again. I even managed to simulate the sensation of being up against a deadline I was in imminent danger of missing (in fact, that last bit was not difficult at all, as my editor at Routledge would be able to confirm). I hope that the result of all this will be that the advice below will be as relevant and realistic as possible. It is not just an abstract exercise. I will try not simply to tell you 'do this' and 'don't do that' without any reference to the practical reality of student life. Rather, this book is based on my own real experience of trying to complete exactly the tasks with which you, as an undergraduate student, will be confronted.

However, perhaps the most useful parts of this book arise from my recent experience lecturing and examining on undergraduate courses. I can offer you a lecturer's-eye view of the academic world. What are lecturers really looking for in student presentations and essays? What mistakes in student essays really annoy them? What are the most common and the most annoying of all? What sort of questions do lecturers like to hear in their seminars and classes? What do lecturers look for when they are marking exams? How can you make your exam script stand out from the rest? How can you play the academic game most successfully?

Romantic geniuses and management consultants

Now, I know this all sounds dreadfully utilitarian and mechanical; even a little Machiavellian. What about natural curiosity, learning for learning's sake, the love of knowledge, the spark of genius? Well, these are all wonderful things, and I have nothing to say against any of them in this book. Your time at university will only be enjoyable and fulfilling if you are driven by curiosity and have a love of knowledge. And I certainly believe in the value of learning for its own sake. An education system that only provided students with strictly necessary and useful information would be a dreadful thing. However, the thirst for knowledge and the spark of creativity are not what this book is about. I am taking it for granted that, like most human beings, you have these things already.

There are many different schools of thought when it comes to the purpose of a university education in subjects in the arts, humanities and social sciences, and the way that a student should approach that education. These cover a spectrum ranging from what could be called the 'romantic genius' view to the 'management consultant' view. The 'romantic genius' view is one that I have come across directly and indirectly on many occasions, especially among students and academics in Oxford and Cambridge. On this view, a university education is an opportunity for intellectually and artistically gifted young people to frolic and flourish in the worlds of literature and learning, devoting themselves to the study of the classics, broadening their philosophical horizons, writing poetry between lectures, living and behaving rather like Oscar Wilde, indulging in clever conversation and Bohemian decadence. On this view, lectures and essay topics might or might not have anything to do with vulgar formalities such as syllabuses and exams; the point of going to lectures, reading books and writing essays is to enrich your soul and quench your thirst for knowledge, not to prepare for exams or get high marks. On this view, then, there are no rules, no practical techniques, no transferable skills; just the love of learning and self-motivated, self-sufficient romantic geniuses of students who may or may not get a first at the end of it all, depending on just how brilliantly they happen to perform in their final exams. The first-class student has an extra *je ne sais quoi* to which the non-genius cannot and need not aspire.

As you might be able to detect from my tone, I do not myself subscribe to the 'romantic genius' view. What about the other extreme, the 'management consultant' view? This is a brutally analytic and strictly utilitarian approach to learning. It says: this task can be broken down into several sub-tasks; we can analyse these sub-tasks and the resources available to complete them; there are set rules and logical procedures that we need to identify and then follow; once we have done this we will be able to produce the desired outcome – a first. On this view, then, lectures, reading, classes and essays are simply sub-tasks within the overall task of getting high marks, in order to get a good degree, in order to acquire transferable skills, which, in turn, will be attractive to employers and enable you to earn a high salary, perhaps as a management consultant.

You will already have gathered that my own views are somewhat closer to the 'management consultant' view than to the 'romantic genius' view. However, I have presented both views in an extreme and caricatured way. Of course, the ideal lies somewhere in between, and it will be up to you to decide where. One of the reasons why I decided to write this book, however, was in order to undermine a particular part of the 'romantic genius' view of university life, namely the part that says only geniuses get firsts, and there's nothing that non-geniuses can do to understand how they do it, or to emulate the achievement.

In five or six years supervising undergraduates in Cambridge, I have only ever taught one or two students who I felt were so gifted that they might be termed 'geniuses'. We have all probably come across a few such individuals, who seem to have intellectual and creative gifts that are quite out of the ordinary. However, even in those cases, you can be sure that what appears to be a certain level of 'genius' was in fact the result of years of practice and hard work. Even supposing that geniuses exist, how many university students fall into that category? One in a hundred thousand? One in a thousand? Let's suppose it is as many as one in a hundred. So, 1 per cent of students are geniuses. But 10 per cent of students get firsts. This book, then, is for non-geniuses who want to be among that other 9 per cent of students who get firsts.

In my experience, both as a student and as a lecturer, it is fairly unusual to come across a student who says that they hope to get a first in their degree. There are three possible reasons for this, I think: modesty, lack of ambition, or lack of self-belief. Modest students might think it presumptuous even to talk about the possibility of their getting a first, while secretly harbouring the hope that they will. Unambitious students don't want to get a first; they are happy setting their sights on an upper second. Others believe that only geniuses get firsts and so think there is no point in them even trying. I don't know whether you fall into any of those categories. But I hope that this book will persuade you that it is worth trying to get a first, while also giving you the information you need to go about doing so (whether you are a genius or not).

Chapter 2

Taking aim

The task and the resources

Summary

If you want to hit the target, you need to know where it is. Make sure you understand the basic structure of your course. Look at old exam papers and course documentation in order to establish how each course you are taking is examined and how your work will be evaluated. Work out what the key questions are for each course and what the range of possible answers is. Identify the resources available to help you hit the target. Your two most valuable resources are your own time and your teachers. Manage your time. Manage your teachers.

Taking the first step

The first step towards getting a first in your degree is getting clear about what the rules of the game are and how to play by them successfully. You have already made a good start by buying this book! The next thing to do, once you have finished reading it, is to ask one or more of your lecturers or tutors directly what they think you need to do if you want to get a first in your degree. They will be only too pleased to give you advice. It looks good for them and the department too if their students get high marks. Indeed, this is probably the single most important and encouraging fact to take on board at the outset: *your teachers really want you to do well and get high marks*. Most departments are absolutely falling over themselves to give more first-class marks if they possibly can (so long as you stay in their good books). Reading the rest of this book will tell you how to make it as easy as possible for your lecturers' dreams to come true in your case, by making sure you are one of the students to whom they feel justified in awarding a first-class degree.

Knowledge is power

The key to success in many tasks is proper preparation. When decorating a room in your house, for example, the key to success is cleaning, repairing, filling and sanding the walls, ceilings and wood-work before you start to decorate. If you are laying a floor, you have to make sure the surface is absolutely level before you start. The key to academic success is also proper preparation. As we will see when we come to look at specific skills like essay-writing in later chapters, you can only hope to make efficient use of your time if you identify the key components of the task (reading, noting, planning, writing) and estimate how much time you have available for each. The same sort of process can be applied to your entire degree. This preparatory identification of the key tasks in front of you and the resources available to help you undertake them can be broken down into three main categories: understanding the structure of your degree; iden-tifying the ways your work is assessed; and identifying the range of resources available to you. In summary, knowledge is power! If you know what is expected of you and what help is available, you are well on your way to achieving success.

This may seem incredibly obvious, but you would be surprised how many students, even when the deadlines for assessed work are fast approaching, or their end-of-year exams are just around the corner, still have not looked properly at the course documentation and so do not know what the key issues are, what questions are likely to come up in the exam, what the word limit for their assessed work is, and so on. The reason for this is sometimes disorganisation, sometimes laziness. More often, though, I think it is an ostrich-like response to the fear of failure. If you don't even think about the stressful event of being assessed or examined then you won't need to face up to that fear. This strategy works in one way – it delays the dreaded moment of realising the extent of the task. In another way, however, it is a dreadful strategy, since realising the extent of the task is an essential prerequisite to completing it successfully. Don't be an ostrich. Find out exactly what is being asked of you, what the essay topics are, how much you will need to read, what the exam will be about; and find all this out at the *very start of the academic year*.

Understand the structure of your degree

It will be down to your lecturers to explain the details of your particular degree programme to you, and you will certainly be given plenty of guidance on whatever course choices you have to make, and on the modes of assessment for each course. So, what I will offer here is a brief, basic and general introduction to the sorts of questions to bear in mind.

Different degrees at different universities are organised in different ways. Many universities now have a two-semester system rather than the old three-term system. And increasingly degrees are examined by assessed coursework instead of or as well as by exams. There is also a trend for more students to take combined honours courses, studying several different subjects rather than just one. For example, you might be taking a degree in French and business, or politics and philosophy, or English and Latin, or history and sociology, or film and American history.

Your programme of study will probably have some compulsory elements (especially in the first year) and a range of further 'courses' or 'papers', of which you will have to choose to take a certain number each year. These are the modules which, together, comprise the teaching and assessment for your degree. If you are taking the first year of a degree in English literature, for example, there might be compulsory courses on Shakespeare and the history of the English language; and then you might be given a range of further courses on poetry, drama and novels from different periods and places, from which to choose one or two.

Whatever the basic pattern of your course, the following are the key questions you need to answer for yourself right at the start of your degree

- How is my degree structured?
- Does each year count equally towards my final degree? Or are some years (such as the first year) less important?
- How many courses do I need to take each term/semester/year?
- How many credits is each course worth?
- How is each course examined? By exam or by coursework?

- When are the deadlines/exams? Are they at the end of the term/ semester or at the end of the year, or some other time?
- What is the best way to spread my workload over the course of the term/semester/year?
- Is attendance at the lectures, classes or seminars for each course compulsory or voluntary?
- Do some courses involve a much greater time commitment than others?
- Which courses seem to offer the most credit for the least time commitment?

The last questions on this list suggest a particularly utilitarian approach to your studies. Hopefully the love of your subject and your interest in particular courses will be the main motivations in making course choices. But, all other things being equal, it is certainly at least worth thinking about the amount of time that each course will require and whether some offer particularly efficient uses of your time. It is always a very good idea to ask students in the year above you how they found each course: Which are the most stimulating? Which ones have a reputation for being extremely demanding? Which require most preparation for classes and seminars?

Identify methods of assessment

The course documentation that you are provided with at the start of your degree will tell you how each paper or course is assessed. Do not assume that all courses are assessed the same way. The following are the six main ways students are assessed:

- Attendance (a certain level of attendance may be required at lectures and classes before you can be deemed to have passed a particular course)
- Language exercises and oral examination (for language students)
- Oral presentation
- Coursework essay
- Written examination
- Dissertation (an extended piece of written work offered instead of a whole course, normally in the final year of your degree).

It is worth paying attention to how each course is assessed. If you do have a choice, you might want to think about whether, on balance, you tend to do better in exams or in coursework essays. Perhaps it would make sense to try to choose courses with a mixture of assessment methods, so that you spread the load over the year between coursework and exams. Concentrating exclusively on one or the other could lead to an inactive year and a very stressful exam period or a relaxed exam period but a generally high level of stress the rest of the year. If you are terrified of public speaking then you can decide whether or not now is the time to overcome that fear by taking a course in which you will have to give an assessed presentation (see Chapter 8).

Identify the available resources

Your university and your department will organise 'induction' events for you at the start of the year. These will introduce you to the resources that will be at your disposal for the duration of your degree course, to support you in your studies. Three of the most important of these are:

- Lectures, classes and seminars
- Libraries – for books and journal articles
- Online resources.

The lectures, classes and seminars that your department organises are the starting point for your studies. These will identify the basic questions that are considered important in each subject and orient you in relation to major primary and secondary reading material (see 'Primary and secondary material' below, and Chapter 3). Getting the most out of the library or libraries available to you is of the utmost importance if you want to produce excellent work (see Chapter 4). It is also important to identify, with help from lecturers and librarians, what the internet can and cannot be profitably used for in your areas of interest (see Chapter 6).

The two most valuable resources at your disposal are your time and your lecturers. I will come back to these at the end of this chapter.

Primary and secondary material

The distinction made in the previous paragraph between primary and secondary material is fundamental in all arts, humanities and social science degrees. It will probably be taken for granted by your lecturers and it is crucial that you grasp its significance.

Primary material means different things in different disciplines. In history, it means documents such as first-hand accounts and contemporary newspaper reports of important events; autobiographies and letters of notable individuals; political speeches, periodical publications, photographs, and artefactual pieces of 'material culture', from scientific instruments to kitchen utensils. If you are studying literature, then primary material means original compositions by major poets, playwrights and novelists. In philosophy, too, primary material means important writings by major thinkers. In social sciences such as sociology, psychology and anthropology, primary material includes both empirical case studies and classic theoretical treatises.

Primary material is the currency of the academic world. To be taken seriously as an academic you have to write about primary material that you have discovered, produced or scrutinised yourself at first hand. This material could be the racy, previously undiscovered correspondence of a seventeenth-century clergyman; or a new statistical analysis of suicide rates amongst sociology students; or the published works of a major philosopher or poet. Whatever it is, the articles or books that you write about this primary material themselves constitute secondary material. And it is this secondary material, which summarises, interprets and comments upon primary material and other secondary texts, which is most often the starting point for students. Your reading lists will, more often than not, be made up predominantly of secondary texts.

Secondary material is much more plentiful than the primary material it is based upon. Shakespeare's complete works, for instance, which certainly qualify as primary texts, can be fitted into one large volume (I know this, because I received it free when I joined a book club a few years ago). The same could not be said of all the secondary material (commentaries, interpretations, discussions, speculations, hypotheses) that has been written about Shakespeare. This would run into many thousands of volumes. Entering 'Shakespeare' in the 'subject' field of the online catalogue for the British Library, for instance, results in almost 16,000 hits.[1] This only covers books published in Britain. Doing the same thing with the online catalogue of the American equivalent – the Library of Congress – produces the message 'Your

---

1 British Library Public Catalogue: <http://blpc.bl.uk> (accessed 5 January 2004).

search retrieved more records than can be displayed. Only the first 10,000 will be shown'.[2] If you were to add studies written in all languages – as well as journal articles – the amount of material would increase even more dramatically. In short, secondary interpretations and discussions of primary material (especially of important primary material such as Shakespeare's plays, or the Bible, or Plato's dialogues, or Newton's laws, or the American constitution, or Marx and Engels' *Communist Manifesto*, or Freud's case studies) multiply almost indefinitely. Each new study spawns reviews, reactions and responses from an international community of academic experts. And it is the job of your poor lecturers to select a few items from this sprawling mass of academic literature to help introduce you to the subject. One of the reasons why your lecturers are such a valuable resource is their ability to guide you through the forest of secondary literature by providing you with well-chosen items on your reading lists.

Nonetheless, the fact remains that primary material is what it is all about. Secondary texts exist to help you understand primary material, not for their own sake. Your lecturers will doubtless guide you towards the most important primary texts for the subject they are teaching you. I know from my own experience of teaching historical topics that reading primary texts with students in seminars provides a sense of the experience of a particular aspect of life in a particular time and place in a way that no amount of summarising secondary material can ever do. If, for some reason, it does not become clear to you what the most useful primary texts are, in relation to a given topic, it is important to ask. 'What is the most important primary material for this topic?' is a question that, when asked politely and in the right circumstances, will make you appear interested and intelligent, and one that your lecturer will be pleased to answer.

The most important thing for you to know is that, from a lecturer's point of view, there is a very clear distinction between first-class student work and competent student work, which relates to this distinction between primary and secondary material. First-class essays show a command of primary material. Merely competent essays tend to rely on the sorts of summaries and generalisations found in secondary texts. When reading a first-class essay, you are left in no doubt that its author has read the primary texts and thought carefully

2 Library of Congress Online Catalog: <http://catalog.loc.gov> (accessed 5 January 2004).

about which sections to refer to and quote from. When reading an essay of upper- or lower-second standard, it is not quite clear whether the student has looked at any primary material at all or has simply made judicious use of secondary sources. If you are short of time when reading in preparation for a presentation, essay or exam, then, one of the most useful things you can do, very often, is to spend the remaining time reading (or rereading) the relevant primary texts.

Manage your time

As I said above, your two most valuable resources are your time and your teachers. Making the transition from school to university, as I mentioned in Chapter 1, involves taking responsibility for your own programme of study and taking the initiative. One of the most difficult parts of this is learning to manage your time effectively. You will have a lot of demands on your time, including some or all of the following:

- Academic work
- Paid work
- Socialising and going out
- Recovering from socialising and going out
- Sport
- Student politics
- Other student societies
- Coffee, tea and sympathy with friends
- Relationships
- Religion.

Managing all these demands on your time is very difficult. Depending on how your degree programme is organised, you will have quite a lot of unstructured time during which, if you wanted, you could do nothing at all. This would be a bad idea, for many reasons (including the risk of becoming depressed). Don't be an ostrich. Look ahead through the whole year and identify when the important deadlines for your work come. If you have two pieces of assessed work due to be handed in at the end of March, say, don't leave them both till then – one will have to be done by January or February to leave time for the second. At the start of the academic year work out how much work you have to do over the whole year, and decide how to spread it out appropriately and how to balance it with paid work and other commitments. There may be one course that involves a lot of preparation for the class on a week-to-week basis. Do not let this prevent you doing work on other courses for which the deadlines seem a long way off. They won't stay a long way off for long. Do not leave all your revision until the week or two before the exams. By keeping organised notes and looking over them periodically through the year, you can make sure that you are well prepared for the exams even before your final period of revision (see Chapter 11).

Well, it's very easy for me to give you all these sensible dos and don'ts, but how can you achieve this in practice? I know from experience how overwhelming student life can be. At times it seems impossible to cope with – for instance, a hangover, a disintegrating relationship, a nine o'clock lecture, a shift at work, and an approaching essay deadline all at the same time: should you go to the library, go to the lecture, go to work, or go back to bed? There are no simple answers, but there are some techniques you can use to make your life a little more manageable.

The same principle applies to managing your time as to understanding your degree: knowledge is power. The reason why things get to a stage where they seem overwhelming and unmanageable is that we can't face even thinking about them and so let them build up until we can't ignore them any longer, by which time there is a real crisis. It is important, therefore, to have a clear idea of the main demands on your time from the outset. Let's suppose you are going to be kind to yourself and have the weekend completely free from all kinds of work. The remaining five days contain 120 hours. Allowing you 8 hours' sleep a night, that leaves 80 waking hours in the week. You will need, say, 3 hours a day for meals and coffee breaks. And let's allow a further 2 hours a day for travelling between home, university and work, and back. That leaves 55 hours. Suppose that you have 10 hours of lectures and classes a week, and that you do 10 hours of paid work. That still leaves 35 hours. How do you want to break that time up? How many evenings during the week do you want to do academic work or paid work? How many do you want to stay in or go out? How many hours do you spend on football or politics or writing for the student newspaper? If you have figures in mind for all these activities, you will be starting from a position of knowledge. You could even draw a pie-chart of your time and divide it into appropriately sized segments to give you a visual representation. If you have calculated that you can afford a certain number of evenings off per week, you can enjoy them to the full, rather than spend them worrying about what else you should be doing. The ideal to aim for (which few of us ever achieve) is to be completely focused on what you are doing while you are doing it, without worrying about other things you have or have not done yet.

Time-management technology

The three key pieces of technology to help you with time management are the timetable, the diary and the list. A weekly timetable helps you visualise your week and, like a well-kept appointments diary, helps you make sure you have a clear idea of your main commitments each week. Lists of 'things to do' are also helpful. If you are feeling overwhelmed by different demands on your time, writing them all down helps to gain a sense of control over your life, especially once you start crossing them off. You can then decide which are the most urgent tasks and when you have time available to deal with them. You can then use your diary to mark out blocks of time for them. Lists like this should include items such as spending time talking to friends and time just taking care of yourself.

Break big tasks down into little tasks

The single most effective way to make big academic tasks seem more manageable is to break them down into their components. If you have an assessed essay to write, for instance, that can be broken down into a lot of smaller sub-tasks, none of which, on its own, seems quite so daunting. The way the chapters of this book are divided up indicates exactly what the sub-tasks of any academic task might be: going to the relevant lectures, finding the right reading material, reading and taking notes, doing extra research using the internet, planning your essay, and writing your essay.

Manage your teachers

After your time, your next most valuable academic resource is your teachers. To put it very simply, right at the outset: students who get firsts are those who have worked out what their lecturers are looking for. Your lecturers are a valuable resource not just because of the knowledge and guidance that they can offer you, but also because they are the people who decide which work gets first-class marks and which does not. If your lecturers like you, notice that you take an interest in their subject, and can see that you are working hard, they will very much hope that you get a first. Although assessed work will almost always be anonymous – so your lecturers will probably not know who wrote which essay – it is in your interest to get on well with your lecturers and work out what they want.

There is a delicate balance to be struck here. One of the things that lecturers least like to see in student essays is their own lectures regurgitated. As I will explain in the next chapter, the point of lectures is not to give you the answers but to alert you to the important questions. What a lecturer wants to see is that you are interested in their course and that you have learned to see – *for yourself* – why the questions it raises are so important. Up to a point, this involves mimicking your lecturer. But what you are mimicking is not what she actually says in lectures, but her *style* of thought, and her way of asking questions. Perhaps the most pleasing sort of essay to receive as a lecturer is one that does all these things but disagrees with the interpretation that you favour yourself. Intelligent dissent may be a more effective form of flattery than anything else.

Lecturers, as I have said, want to see that you are thinking for yourself. This means developing your own voice. This is not the same thing, as I mentioned in Chapter 1, as simply having personal preferences and personal opinions. It means developing a certain way of thinking about the evidence; making the material your own; making the questions your own. Students who get firsts tend to have a strong voice of their own, and to have a 'line' that they take on important questions in their subject. This is something that you can only develop by careful reading and thinking and analysis of the evidence. Then you will be able to say, with intelligent reasons, what you think the strengths and weaknesses are of the different trends in recent feminist literary criticism; or whether or not you think the French Revolution achieved its aims of increasing liberty, equality and fraternity; or whether or not the 'Renaissance' is a helpful historical category; or whether the problem of evil is an insurmountable obstacle to belief in God, and so on. You need your own arguments, your own evidence, your own persuasive techniques, not just your own opinions (and not just knowledge about what other people think).

Making use of tutorial time

There are two main ways that you will come into contact with your lecturers: in lectures, classes and seminars; and in one-to-one meetings to discuss your work. Behaving attentively and helpfully in lectures and seminars is an important part of your relationship with your lecturers. They will notice these things. This is covered in Chapter 3.

One-to-one tutorial time with your lecturers is one of the most valuable resources available to you if you want to do well. If you are studying at Oxford or Cambridge, you will have more of this sort of time available to you. But wherever you are studying, lecturers will have 'office hours' when they are available to talk to you about your work; and you will probably also have a 'tutor' who is responsible more broadly for taking an academic and pastoral concern in your welfare. Make as much use as possible of tutorial time. It offers you a chance to understand what your lecturers really find interesting in their subject and, thus, a chance to increase your own understanding of how to get a first.

It is a good idea to think, in advance, about what you hope to get out of your tutorial contact with lecturers or tutors, both generally and in particular instances. The particular instances are likely to be related to assessed work you are currently preparing – whether that be a presentation, an essay or a dissertation. Spend some time preparing for these meetings by thinking about which aspects of the topic gave you trouble or particularly interested you, and what questions would be the most useful ones to ask – maybe make a list for yourself of some of these questions. The purpose of tutorial meetings is to have a two-way discussion about your ideas. Make sure that you get your say, and that you take a hand in guiding the discussion in the ways that would be most helpful for you.

Take notes of the important parts of what you and your lecturer say during your meeting. These notes will provide a record of the way that your thoughts developed during the conversation – and of any new facts or ideas with which your lecturer furnished you – which will be invaluable when it comes to revising for your exams.

Of course, you do not need to write down every word that you and your lecturer say – use your discretion about what to write down, and when. For example, if you are having a particularly animated and engaging conversation, it's probably best not to keep interrupting the flow of it to write things down. But you could, perhaps, at a convenient pause in the conversation, ask your lecturer if they could give you a couple of minutes to note down what you have just been talking about. Another possibility is making some notes immediately after the meeting, while the issues you discussed are still fresh in your mind.

The thing to have in mind all the while is that understanding what your lecturer thinks are interesting questions, important evidence, and valid ways of arguing is a crucially important part of working out how to get a first.

Chapter 3

Lectures, classes and seminars

Summary

Lectures are an efficient use of your time. They give you access to one of the most useful resources at your disposal at university – your lecturers. To make the most of them you need to learn how to take notes in lectures effectively and selectively. The point of lectures is to raise important questions and guide your reading, not to provide you with definitive answers. Classes and seminars give you an opportunity to discuss material in more depth, experiment with your own ideas, and make a good impression on your lecturers.

Active learning

University teaching and learning differs from what you experienced at school. The teaching comes in longer chunks (normally 50 or 60 minutes at a time), and more of it is in a non-interactive lecture format. The trend, however, is towards providing more classes and seminars and somewhat fewer lectures. In this chapter I will distinguish between lectures on the one hand and classes and seminars on the other. I do not distinguish between classes and seminars, but use the terms interchangeably to indicate a session that involves more interaction, student participation and discussion.

I can tell, from the way many of my students look during my lectures, that they think of these as entirely passive occasions from their point of view. And, from consultation with colleagues, I have learned that it is not that my lectures are particularly boring – all lecturers have noticed this tendency for many students to seem passive during lectures. Looking passive and bored during your lectures will make your lecturers feel unhappy, which I am sure is something you do not want. It also indicates a misconception about how to get the most out of lectures.

There is a distinction to be made between non-interactive and interactive forms of teaching and learning. Lectures are almost entirely non-interactive. You and the lecturer do not have a discussion. You might ask a question or two, which the lecturer will answer, but, for the most part, the lecturer does the talking. However, this distinction between interactive and non-interactive is not a distinction between active and passive forms of learning. In a lecture, you should be actively listening, thinking, and taking notes. You can learn actively in lectures as well as in seminars and classes.

Polite learning

I can't believe I really have to spell out the advice in this section, but several colleagues suggested that I should include it in this book, so here goes. Lectures, classes and seminars are occasions on which you have the opportunity to make a good impression on your lecturers as an interested and able student. They are also opportunities for you to make a bad impression. If you want to do well in your degree, it is not normally a good idea to annoy your lecturers. In lectures and seminars you should behave attentively and politely. The following is a list of fairly obvious things *not* to do in lectures. If you want to be polite and stay in your lecturers' good books, do not:

- Behave like a naughty schoolchild (sitting at the back giggling and passing notes)
- Have a private conversation with the person next to you
- Stare out of the window and pay no attention
- Sleep
- Send or receive text messages
- Make phone calls
- Eat your lunch
- Smoke.

Lectures

Lectures are a prime opportunity for you to do some detective work on your lecturers. They are bound to reveal a lot of their likes and dislikes, enthusiasms and aversions, prejudices and preferences in their lectures. Look out for these; their importance and significance was explained in the last section of Chapter 2, 'Manage your teachers', pages 29–32.

What are lectures for?

Obviously, I cannot presume to speak for all lecturers in all subjects. Your own lecturers will have their own ideas about what they hope you will get out of their lectures. I expect that, for the most part, however, they would agree with the following general principles.

First of all, let's get clear about what lectures are *not* for. The point of a lecture is not to tell you everything you need to know about a topic. Nor is it to give you the answers to the sorts of questions that you will be asked to address in assessed presentations, essays or exams. Lectures are not a primary or a secondary source: they should not be quoted in essays. What, then, are lectures for? There are four main things they might do:

- Provide you with a *big picture* and background information on the subject
- Identify and contextualise the most important *primary materials*
- Identify scholarly *debates* you will come across in the secondary literature
- Provide you with *key questions* to bear in mind when reading.

So, for instance, I give a course of lectures on 'Science and religion in nineteenth-century Britain'. In those lectures, I do not aim to give students answers to questions such as 'Was there a conflict between science and religion in the nineteenth century?'. Instead, I hope to give them the information they need in order to research the questions further themselves and form their own judgement. This involves:

- Explaining the big picture – why have people thought that the relationship between science and religion in this period is interesting?
- Providing background information – what were the most import- ant scientific and religious developments and debates of the period?
- Identifying and providing extracts from primary materials, in this case works of science, philosophy and theology of the period.
- Explaining which historians have favoured a 'conflict' model, and which a more harmonious model of science–religion

relationships in this period, and why; recommending important secondary texts.

- Suggesting that students, when reading primary and secondary texts, keep in mind questions such as 'Which science?', 'Whose religion?', 'When?' and 'Where?', rather than resting content with broad generalisations.

Most of your lectures will be designed with comparable aims in mind. An introductory course on Shakespeare, for instance, would not try to teach you one single way of thinking about Shakespeare, nor to provide you with definitive answers about the meanings of individual plays. Instead, your lectures would give you background information on the circumstances of production and reception of the plays and poetry; give you information about their social and political contexts; explain some of the leading critical approaches to Shakespeare; and equip you with some questions to ask yourself about literary and dramatic devices and their uses when reading the texts for yourself.

Lectures will provide you with key questions, the resources to answer them, and even some potential answers to evaluate. However, they will not tell you all you need to know and they will not give you definitive answers.

Lecture handouts

An important part of any lecture is the handout, which your lecturer will provide. This will probably give you an outline of the topics that the lecture will cover; some key terms, names, or dates; and a reading list. Keep your handouts for future reference. They will come in useful when you need to be reminded of basic information on a topic. Most importantly of all, they will provide you with a list of the books and articles that your lecturer thinks are most useful for this topic. One of the main points of lectures is to offer you orientation and guidance about what to read and what to look for when you read it. The reading list will contain the information you need to start that next stage of the process (which we will come on to in Chapter 4).

Lectures are good for you

Most of the lectures offered on undergraduate courses these days are very good, others are a little boring, and a very few are, perhaps, not so good. However, even your less interesting lectures will provide you with invaluable information about the subjects you are studying and, almost as importantly, about the questions that your lecturer thinks are important and the ways of answering them that he thinks are most productive.

The point about lectures is that they save you massive amounts of time. In a period of around 50 minutes or so you will be presented with an amount of information and analysis that would have taken you (and did take the lecturer) many hours, weeks, or even years to accumulate and organise.

Taking notes in lectures

Efficient note-taking is an important skill to develop both when doing reading for an essay (see Chapter 5) and when attending lectures and seminars. You will need to develop your own preferred method, finding a way to write down enough so that you remember the points that the lecturer was making and any important examples, names or dates the lecturer mentioned (although often the lecture handout can serve this purpose to a large extent), but not so much that you don't have time really to take in and attend to the lecturer's arguments. Even if you think that you are taking everything in, understanding it, and will be able to recall it: don't be so sure. You would be amazed how quickly the contents of lectures can vanish entirely from your memory. A final reason to take notes during your lectures is to make your poor lecturers happy. I can tell you from experience that it is quite unnerving delivering a lecture and seeing some students sit through the whole thing not taking any notes at all. 'Surely, *some* of this is worth writing down', I think to myself as I notice a student, with arms crossed, impassive and unimpressed, staring resolutely either out of the window or, most unnerving of all, straight at me, for the duration of the lecture, while not even having taken out a pad of paper or a pen. Even the least exciting lectures will provide you with important guidance about the reading and thinking you will have to do for yourself. Much of this guidance will be worth noting down.

While taking no notes at all might disappoint your lecturer and leave you ill equipped for the researching, thinking and writing that lie ahead, the opposite extreme of trying to note down everything the lecturer says is equally ill advised. Unless you are an unusually gifted speed-writer, or trained in shorthand, or have lecturers who speak tediously slowly, you will not be able to note down every word the lecturer says. Instead you have to get into the habit of selective note-taking. The things to look out for are indications your lecturer gives of what she thinks are:

- The most important primary texts
- The most important secondary texts
- Secondary texts that are important but wrong
- The most interesting scholarly disputes
- The least interesting disputes
- Questions that are worth thinking about
- Questions that are not worth thinking about
- Clichés and misleading caricatures about the subject that should be avoided at all costs
- Other common mistakes that are to be avoided.

You will also have an opportunity at the end of the lecture (or in the middle, if your lecturer has indicated that she does not mind being interrupted) to ask questions about any of the above, or about anything you did not quite understand. Most lecturers will be delighted to be asked questions. This indicates that students were not only listening to the lecture but were sufficiently awake and stimulated by it to ask a further question. Asking questions will make your lecturer happy and mark you out as a conscientious and interested student (unless you ask really difficult questions all the time; or are aggressive in the way you ask them; or interrupt constantly; or refuse to be satisfied by their answer even on the second or third attempt).

Classes and seminars

As I indicated above, I am using the phrase 'classes and seminars' to refer to interactive sessions, which may or may not start with a mini-lecture from the lecturer, but which centre around student presentations, contributions and discussions. For the rest of this chapter I will refer to these just as 'seminars'. Very often these will be focused on a particular text or texts that have been assigned. One or more students might have been asked to give a presentation on the text as the starting point for a group discussion. The seminar will be led either by one of your lecturers or by someone else, perhaps a PhD student or a post-doctoral researcher in your department who is also employed to assist with undergraduate teaching. I will assume in what follows, however, that the seminars are being run by the main lecturer for the course. This will be the case more often than not. I am also assuming in what follows that the seminars, and any presentations you may make in them, are not assessed. I will deal with assessed presentations in Chapter 8.

What are seminars for? There are four main things:

- Developing your analytical *reading* skills (of either primary or secondary texts)
- *Experimenting* with your own ideas in a group discussion
- Developing your *communication* skills
- Pursuing questions and asking for further *guidance* from your lecturer.

Let's imagine you are taking a course on the Italian Renaissance and the set reading for the seminar is an extract from an English translation of the Swiss historian Jacob Burckhardt's classic work, *The Civilisation of the Renaissance in Italy*, which first came out in German in 1860. You have been asked to give a five-minute presentation on the text to get the group discussion going.

Before you start reading the text, you need to know why you have been asked to read it. It will not have been selected carelessly or at random. In this case, in fact, your lecturer has explained to you that this is considered to be one of the most important texts in establishing the Renaissance as a distinct period of time in European history. You get the impression from your lecturer that this is thought to be a Bad Thing. You might decide, therefore, in order to be provocative and to stimulate debate, to read the text looking out for its strengths and thinking about what is most persuasive in the way it tries to distinguish the Renaissance as a distinct period. On the other hand, you might decide to play it safe and think about what is wrong with the text and what is misleading about describing the Renaissance this way. You can have a *provisional* conclusion in mind about the text before you have read a single word of it (note the stress on *provisional*).

The questions that you should be asking yourself about the text will vary depending on, amongst other things, whether it is a primary text or a secondary one. This particular case is an interesting example since it could be seen as either. It is a primary text from one point of view: it is an example of a text produced in a different period and context (nineteenth-century Switzerland); it is considered a 'classic' in its field and worthy of scrutiny and attention; it would be worth thinking carefully about questions of authorship and audience (what was the significance of Burckhardt being a Protestant, for instance?). However, it is a secondary text from another point of view: it is a (relatively) recent discussion by a historian of materials produced several centuries earlier; it is a contribution to a secondary debate about the interpretation of primary sources. You will need to think carefully about which set of questions you want to focus on. Does your lecturer expect you to approach it as an example of polemical historical writing, or as a controversial interpretation of the Italian Renaissance, or both? I will have more to say about active reading and the different questions to ask about primary and secondary sources in the next chapter.

I have already said that a characteristic of students who get firsts is that they have a distinct 'line' on important questions. Seminars offer an opportunity to experiment with different lines; to try out different voices in a relatively stress-free, non-assessed environment. You could try defending the view that the Renaissance never happened – that it is an artefact of later historians such as Burckhardt. If other students or your lecturer are able to shoot this argument down very easily, you might have to rethink your line, or think about evidence to bolster your claim in new ways. To get the most out of seminars it is important to think of them as opportunities to experiment with your own ideas as well as occasions to make sure you have understood the contents of set texts.

You might suppose that, from a teaching point of view, running a seminar is easier than giving a lecture. In some universities you certainly get paid more for giving a lecture than for running a seminar. This is quite unfair. Giving a lecture is much easier: you stand up and talk about something you know a lot about for about an hour, then you stop talking and go back to your office. To run a seminar successfully you have to galvanise a group of (sometimes sleepy, sometimes unprepared, sometimes shy or nervous) students into having a conversation, and keep it going for an hour. To do this successfully you need to have thought carefully about what, in the set text, is interesting and controversial, how to make it come to life, how to set it up in a provocative way that will lead to debate, and so on.

Two things follow from this. First, if you are yourself responsible for giving an introductory presentation, you will need to think about how to galvanise your fellow students into having a discussion, and so will need to ask yourself the questions the lecturer normally needs to ask herself. This will provide you with an opportunity to develop your skills of communication and argumentation. When you come to write assessed work it is just as important to think about how to engage and animate your audience. Seminars are a valuable opportunity to get into the habit of thinking about how to make a question come to life in an engaging way. You are not being asked simply to summarise a text, but to stimulate a conversation.

Second, you should be aware that your lecturer will be impressed (and very grateful) if you are able to contribute stimulating, lively and intelligent thoughts to the seminar. She will be particularly impressed if you are armed with direct quotations from the set text to illustrate and support your point of view. Students who get firsts have a distinctive line of their own, and the evidence from primary sources to back it up.

Chapter 4

Libraries and reading lists

Summary

Before you go to the library, work out how much time you have available for each part of the task. Get hold of the required reading material and do an initial survey of it. Be prepared to go beyond your reading list. Use the contents and index of each book to identify the chapter, section, page or paragraph that you need to read. Skim-read to determine which sections will be the most useful.

What not to do

This chapter and the next one are about finding books and articles on a reading list, reading them, and taking notes from them. That all sounds pretty straightforward, but there are plenty of pitfalls that you need to avoid. The most important thing to take on board at the outset is what *not* to do.

*Do **not** go to the library, get the first book on your reading list, open it at the beginning of the set chapter, open your pad of paper, take out your pen, and start taking notes.* This might seem like the most sensible and logical thing to do. It isn't. Before you take out your pen and paper (or open your laptop), before you make any but the most scanty of notes, you need to:

- Work out which books and articles are actually available
- Get hold of them
- Work out which are going to be the most useful for your essay

- Use the contents page and index of books to work out which pages are the most relevant
- Estimate how much time you have for each book and how many pages you can read and note in that time
- Think carefully about your essay question and what sort of evidence will be most useful to you
- Decide what order to read your selected materials in.

Only after you have gone through all these stages (which this chapter covers in some detail) can you move on to the stage of actually reading and taking notes (which is what the next chapter is about).

Getting hold of the material

Using the library

Using a library is not always straightforward. I made the mistake, when I was a fresher, of deciding not to go to the library induction session – it sounded a little boring, to be honest, and, after all, how difficult can taking a book out of a library really be? I regretted that over the next three years as I battled against a cataloguing and searching system in the library that made no sense to me at all. The library is a central academic resource and you need to know how to use it from the outset. In particular you need to know:

- How the catalogue works
- Whether there are different search functions for journals and for books
- How to find out whether an online version of a journal is available
- Which books can be borrowed and which cannot
- How long they can be borrowed for.

Reading lists

Before you set foot in the library, however, you need to know what you are looking for. Your starting point will probably be a reading list either provided for a particular essay or given in a lecture hand-out. The items on your reading list will probably be divided into primary and secondary material; it is possible that they will all be primary or all be secondary, depending on the nature of the topic.

Each secondary text will fall into one of three categories: book, book chapter or journal article.

A book is, well, a book. It might be a 'monograph' – a book where one author develops a single continuous argument over several chapters. Or it might be an edited book containing contributions by several different authors. A book chapter could be a chapter in a monograph or a chapter in an edited collection.

A journal article is likely to be a more focused and specialised piece of academic writing, written with an academic audience in mind. This does not mean that journal articles are necessarily more difficult or obscure than books. They may or may not be. Even if they are, your lecturer will have recommended them for a reason, and you will get a lot of credit for making the effort to get to grips with them. A further attraction of journal articles is that they often include an 'abstract' or 'synopsis' at the outset, helpfully summarising the argument of the entire article, such as the following from the start of an article about the topic of 'inference to the best explanation' in the philosophy of science:

> ABSTRACT. This paper discusses the nature and the status of inference to the best explanation (IBE). We (1) outline the foundational role given IBE by its defenders and the arguments of critics who deny it any place at all; (2) argue that, on the two main conceptions of explanation, IBE cannot be a foundational inference rule; (3) sketch an account of IBE that makes it contextual and dependent on substantive empirical assumptions, much as simplicity seems to be; (4) show how that account avoids the critics' complaints and leaves IBE an important role; and (5) sketch how our account can clarify debates over IBE in arguments for scientific realism.[1]

Having read this helpful summary of the article I might decide that, although this is certainly going to be very helpful reading for my essay, it sounds rather advanced. It might be good, then, to leave this till last, and start by looking for some more basic material on the subject.

To take another example, below is an essay title and reading list on the topic of women's suffrage in Britain.

---

1 Timothy Day and Harold Kincaid, 'Putting inference to the best explanation in its place', *Synthese* **98** (1994), pp. 271–95; quotation from p. 271.

Essay title

Was female enfranchisement in Britain a triumph for feminism or an inevitable development in a democratic state?

Reading list

Primary

*Patricia Hollis (ed.), *Women in Public 1850–1900: Documents of the Victorian Women's Movement* (London: Allen and Unwin, 1979).

*Marie Mulvey Roberts and Tamae Mizuta (eds), *The Suffragists: Towards the Vote* (London: Routledge/Thoemmes, 1995)

Secondary

Barbara Caine, 'Feminism, suffrage and the nineteenth-century English women's movement', *Women's Studies International Forum* 5.6 (1982), pp. 537–50.

*Sandra Stanley Holton, *Feminism and Democracy: Women's Suffrage and Reform Politics in Britain, 1900–1918* (Cambridge: Cambridge University Press, 1986).

*Sandra Stanley Holton, 'Women and the vote', in June Purvis (ed.), *Women's History: Britain 1850–1945: An Introduction* (London: Routledge, 2000), pp. 277–305.

Maroula Joannou and June Purvis (eds), *The Women's Suffrage Movement: New Feminist Perspectives* (Manchester: Manchester University Press, 1998).

*Martin Pugh, *The March of Women: A Revisionist Analysis of the Campaign for Women's Suffrage, 1886–1914* (Oxford: Oxford University Press, 2002).

June Purvis and Sandra Stanley Holton (eds), *Votes for Women* (London: Routledge, 2000).

In this example, the primary sources are clearly separated at the top of the reading list. It is crucial that you look at these, but possibly best to do so after you have some idea of what you will be arguing in your essay (see the section in Chapter 5 on 'Active reading', pages 59–61). Of the secondary sources, the first, by Barbara Caine, is a journal article. The title of the journal is given in italics: *Women's Studies International Forum*. The particular one that you want is volume 5, number 6 (which is what '5.6' means), published in 1982.

Sandra Stanley Holton's book *Feminism and Democracy* is a mono-graph; so is Martin Pugh's *The March of Women*. Holton's piece called 'Women and the vote' is a chapter in an edited book. The other two entries are both edited books. In this case, the lecturer has marked some of the items with an asterisk to indicate that they are particularly important. You should start with these, but perhaps be prepared to rely on the non-asterisked items if the first-choice texts are unavailable for some reason.

The reading list above also helps to illustrate two useful tips on how to make efficient use of your time. First, you will notice that there are two items by the same author – Sandra Stanley Holton – a book, and a chapter in an edited book. The chapter is published later than the book. Holton will have condensed and summarised some of the most important points in her book for the shorter chapter. This does not mean you should not look at the book at all, but rather that it might make sense to start with the later book chapter to get an overview of the topic and a flavour of Holton's argument before using the book for some more detailed material. You will find that this happens very often: an author of an important and influential monograph will subsequently be invited to contribute to edited collections, for which purpose they will provide a condensed version of the argument of their book. Be on the look-out for this pattern, and make use of the later condensations of an author's work.

A second, rather more incidental tip is about making use of online booksellers as a resource in identifying what books to read. The American website for the booksellers Amazon, for instance, provides a facility for looking inside many books – especially recently published ones. This facility allows you to see the contents page, the index and, sometimes, a sample few pages of the text of the book. This is particularly helpful in the case of edited books that your lecturer has put on a reading list without offering any indication of which chapters are most relevant. So, in the example above, the lecturer has listed *Votes for Women* edited by Purvis and Holton but not specified any particular chapters. Going to the amazon.com website and searching for the book, I find that I can look inside it and, having looked at the full table of contents, might decide that Chapter 2, 'The ideas of British suffragism', by Christine Bolt, looks helpful.[2] Or I might

---

2 Note that this facility is not currently offered on the British site (http://www.amazon.co.uk), but only on the American one: <http://www.amazon.com> (accessed 6 January 2004).

decide that none of the chapters looks directly relevant to this particular essay topic, which in itself would be useful information if the
book were unavailable; I could then reassure myself that I was not
missing anything crucial if I could not get hold of it.

Going beyond the reading list when you can't find the books on the list

The place to start may be the reading list that your lecturer has given
you, but that is certainly not the place to stop. You might have
trouble getting hold of some or, in the worst-case scenario, all of the
books and articles that your lecturer has recommended. If it really is
all of them, then it is probably best to e-mail your lecturer and ask
for advice. Otherwise, the thing to do is to use your initiative. Look
for books on the same subject using the library catalogue. Let's
suppose that I had trouble getting hold of most of the above items
about women's suffrage. I would then go to the library catalogue
and type 'women's suffrage' in the 'title' field. If I were at, say,
Birmingham University, I would be offered about 30 titles, which
would come up on the screen looking like this:

1. The march of the women: a revisionist analysis of the
   campaign for women's suffrage, 1866–1914 / Martin Pugh.
   2000
2. The women's suffrage movement in Britain, 1866–1928 /
   Sophia A. van Wingerden. 1999
3. The women's suffrage movement: a reference guide 1866–
   1928 / Elizabeth Crawford. 1999
4. The British women's suffrage campaign, 1866–1928 /
   Harold L. Smith. 1998
5. The women's suffrage movement: new feminist perspectives
   / edited by Maroula Joannou and June Purvis. 1998
6. The men's share?: masculinities, male support and women's
   suffrage in Britain, 1890–1920 / edited by Angela V. John
   and Claire Eustance. 1997
7. Suffrage days: stories from the women's suffrage movement
   / Sandra Stanley Holton. 1996
8. Voices and votes: a literary anthology of the women's
   suffrage campaign / Glenda Norquay. 1995
9. Before the vote was won: arguments for and against
   women's suffrage 1864–1896 / edited by Jane Lewis. 1987

10. Suffrage and the Pankhursts / edited by Jane Marcus. 1987

11. Feminism and democracy: women's suffrage and reform politics in Britain, 1900–1918 / Sandra Stanley Holton. 1986

12. Women at work collection from the Imperial War Museum / Imperial War Museum (Great Britain). 1986

13. Stepping stones to women's liberty: feminist ideas in the women's suffrage movement 1900–1918 / Les Garner. 1984

14. Smashing times: a history of the Irish women's suffrage movement 1889–1922 / Rosemary Cullen Owens. 1984

15. Women's suffrage and social politics in the French Third Republic / Steven C. Hause with Anne R. Kenney. 1984

16. Women's suffrage in Britain, 1867–1928 / Martin Pugh. 1980

17. Separate spheres: the opposition to women's suffrage in Britain / Brian Harrison. 1978

18. One hand tied behind us: the rise of the women's suffrage movement / Jill Liddington and Jill Norris. 1978

19. Feminism and suffrage: the emergence of an independent women's movement in America, 1848–1869 / Ellen Carol DuBois. 1978

20. Women's suffrage and party politics in Britain, 1866–1914 / Constance Rover. 1967

21. Votes and wages: how women's suffrage will improve the economic position of women / A. Maude Rowden. 1914

22. Women's suffrage: a short history of a great movement / Fawcett, Millicent Garrett, Dame, 1847–1929. 1912

23. The suffragette: the history of the women's militant suffrage movement, 1905–1910 / E. Sylvia Pankhurst. 1911

24 Women's suffrage: some sociological reasons for opposing the movement / by Mrs E.M. Simon. 1907

25. Observations on women's suffrage / Viscount Harberton. 1882

26. Address upon women's suffrage in Wyoming, delivered at Association Hall, Philadelphia / Governor John W. Hoyt . . . April 3rd, 1882. 1882

27. Annual report of the Central Committee of the National Society for Women's Suffrage / National Society for Women's Suffrage

28. Annual report of the executive committee of the Manchester National Society for Women's Suffrage / Manchester National Society for Women's Suffrage
29. Annual report – Birmingham Society for Women's Suffrage / Birmingham Society for Women's Suffrage
30. Annual report – Central Committee of the National Society for Women's Suffrage / National Society for Women's Suffrage[3]

That might seem like quite an overwhelming list to grapple with, but the reason I have provided you with the whole list here is in order to illustrate how you could focus in quickly on the titles of a few books to look at. This list includes some items from the original reading list. However, we are assuming that they are not available, so they can be ignored for the sake of this exercise. I have used the catalogue's 'sort' facility and chosen to sort them by 'reverse date', so that the most recently published items come first. There are two reasons for doing this. First, scholarly trends move quite quickly and a secondary text from, for instance, the 1960s or 1970s might (or might not) be rather outdated. Given that you cannot really know, at first glance, whether a work has been superseded or is an unsurpassed classic, it is best to play it safe in the first instance and rely on more recent publications. The second reason for doing this is that the recent discussions will normally offer some sort of overview of previous debates and indicate where their new contribution fits into established categories and discussions. So, let's discount anything published before 1980. Some of the remaining titles are clearly either not relevant to the question (about female enfranchisement in Britain) or sound too specific: this applies to the books specifically about Ireland, France, women at war, and men and masculinities. Deleting these, along with books from the initial reading list and pre-1980 books, leaves nine items:

The women's suffrage movement in Britain, 1866–1928 / Sophia A. van Wingerden. 1999

---

3 I performed this search on the very useful COPAC library catalogue (which covers 24 of the largest university libraries in the UK and Ireland), restricting the search to Birmingham University library: <http://www.copac.ac.uk> (accessed 19 January 2004). For more on using COPAC, see Chapter 6, pages 80–1.

The women's suffrage movement: a reference guide 1866–
1928 / Elizabeth Crawford. 1999

The British women's suffrage campaign, 1866–1928 / Harold
L. Smith. 1998

*Suffrage days: stories from the women's suffrage movement /
Sandra Stanley Holton. 1996

*Voices and votes: a literary anthology of the women's suffrage campaign
/ Glenda Norquay. 1995*

*Before the vote was won: arguments for and against women's suffrage
1864–1896 / edited by Jane Lewis. 1987*

Suffrage and the Pankhursts / edited by Jane Marcus. 1987

Stepping stones to women's liberty: feminist ideas in the
women's suffrage movement 1900–1918 / Les Garner. 1984

*Women's suffrage in Britain, 1867–1928 / Martin Pugh. 1980

Lo and behold – a whole new alternative reading list, which even
includes two books by authors on the original reading list (asterisked),
and three collections of primary sources (in italics). I hope that going
through this rather lengthy example helps to show that all is not lost
if you cannot find the items on your original reading list. I have not
mentioned using the internet or searching for journal articles, both
of which would also be sensible strategies, which I will come on to
in Chapter 6.

Going beyond the reading list out of sheer enthusiasm and conscientiousness

The previous section was about what to do if you are forced into
going beyond the reading list because the material on the list is
unavailable. It is, however, in any case a very good idea to look at
some material that has not been recommended by your lecturer.
Taking the initiative in this way will impress your lecturers and will
also give you a feeling of involvement with the material and responsibility for the task. Only by digging out and reading things for
yourself will you start to get a feel for how to do academic research
and how to assess the relevance and value of material quickly and
effectively. Given that the whole point of this particular skill is using
your own initiative, it would probably be counter-productive for me
to offer you lots of guidance on how to go about it. So, let me
simply suggest the following pointers for how to read around and
beyond the assigned texts for a particular topic:

- Browse the shelves of the library in the vicinity of books given on your reading list.
- Look for alternative collections of primary sources.
- Follow up subjects that grab your interest by chasing up references in the footnotes and bibliography of set readings.
- Trawl through library catalogues, websites, search engines and online journals for promising leads.
- Pursue things you do not understand; be dogged in your search for evidence.

Essays that use ideas and evidence gathered from further reading and research undertaken entirely on the student's own initiative, and presented in an intelligent and persuasive way, are relatively rare. Your lecturers will be predisposed to give such work a first-class mark if they can.

Actively assessing the available time and material

For every piece of written work you undertake, you should work out at the outset how much time you realistically have available for the whole project, including reading, thinking, writing and editing. Think about what proportion of that time should be allotted to each task, as in the following example.

You have to hand in an assessed essay of 2,000 words in about two weeks' time. You estimate that, having subtracted time for lectures, classes, seminars and extra-curricular activities each week, you have about 15 hours available per week. That gives you a total of 30 hours for the whole project. You then need to think about exactly how to divide that time up. You might make the following estimates:

Tracking down books and articles on reading list:	1 hour
Initial survey of materials:	2 hours
Reading and noting:	18 hours
Thinking and planning:	2 hours
Writing first draft:	4 hours
Tutorial discussion with lecturer:	1 hour
Editing, proofreading, and final draft:	2 hours
Total	**30 hours**

If you are a particularly fast writer, you might want to spend more time on reading, noting and thinking, and less time on writing the first and second drafts. Or you might like to save up some of your reading time for after the discussion with your lecturer, if you are able to arrange one. Your lecturer might suggest some good primary or secondary sources that you had missed in your initial reading and noting. Different people will make different decisions about how to divide up the time. But it is essential to go through this process if you want to make the best use of your time.

In the example above, there are 18 hours available for reading and noting. If you imagine that there were six books and articles to look at, that would mean you had about 3 hours per item. If you estimated that you could skim-read at one page per minute, but might take 5 minutes per page on the sections where you were taking fuller notes, then that would give you time to skim-read 120 pages and then go back and make detailed notes on about 12 pages, for each of the six items. (I will come back to skim-reading at the end of this chapter.) Or you might decide, having picked a chapter of about 30 pages, to read and note the whole thing quite carefully. I do not mean to imply that these are standard amounts or rates of reading. Different people work at different rates. And a particularly difficult or important page of a book could take you 20 or 30 minutes to read, reread, re-reread, digest, take notes from, select quotations from and think about. Time yourself to find out how quickly you can skim-read and how long it takes you to make more detailed notes. It is certainly very helpful to have these sorts of calculations in mind so that you know at the outset at least roughly what is a reasonable about of material to try to read, and in how much detail. If you don't do this you will be in danger of taking a disproportionate amount of time over the first book you open and ending up without enough time for the other items on your list. If, as in one of the examples above, you do not have time to make detailed notes on more than 10 or 15 pages of a book, that makes it very important that you choose carefully which pages of which chapters to devote your time to.

I know from my own experience that doing the reading for an essay can sometimes be a frustrating, unproductive and unbelievably slow process. The key to reading is to do it *actively* and *selectively*. Don't approach reading as a passive process in which you simply spectate as page after page of academic text passes before your weary eyes. There are several techniques that can be developed to make your reading more active and selective, and hence more efficient.

Know what you are looking for

At an early stage in your preparation for an essay you should decide (if you have been given a choice) which essay title you are going to write on. A small amount of reading may be necessary to decide this but if you have been to the relevant lectures and seminars you will probably have enough knowledge of the topic to know which aspect you want to study for your essay.

Once you know which title you are going to write on, spend some time really *thinking* about the title; think about each word, and what it means; ask yourself which words in the title are the most important, and which are ambiguous or in need of definition; think about what evidence would be relevant to the question; think about the different possible approaches to the essay, and which one you might favour. You could also break the title down into two or three sub-questions, and then break those down further until you have several basic questions, the answers to which, together, will form the basis of an answer to the question. The following are two examples of how this might work.

Why were there such diverse Christian responses to Darwin's theory of evolution in the nineteenth century?								
What was Darwin's theory of evolution?			**What were the different Christian responses to it?**			**Why were there diverse reactions?**		
Explanation of evolution?	When published?	How different from earlier theories?	'Liberal' Anglicans?	'Conservative' Anglicans?	Non-conformists and Catholics?	Social differences?	Professional affiliations?	Differences in doctrine?

Were the Stoics against the emotions?								
Which Stoics?			**What are the emotions?**			**Why for or against?**		
Greek?	Roman?	Modern?	Difference between emotions and 'passions'?	'Passions' like lust and anger?	Other feelings?	Irrational?	Immoral?	Bodily?

It is essential that you do this sort of analysis before you start reading. This way you will go to the books with a clear set of questions in mind, knowing what material is less relevant and can be skimmed over, and which pages of the books you are reading are the most pertinent and need closer scrutiny. As a general rule, you should not open a book not knowing what you are looking for. If you don't know what you are looking for, you have an extremely small chance of finding it.

Taking stock

Once you have got hold of as many items from your reading list as you can, and, possibly, additional books and articles that you have found for yourself, the next thing to do is take stock of it all. This is the time to skim through the contents pages of books, looking for useful-sounding chapters and sections. Very often the contents page of a book tells you all you need to know. However, if it doesn't, the next place to look is the index.

How to use the index

The index of a book can save you hours of unnecessary and fruitless reading. The first thing to be aware of is that some academic books have more than one index. Several times I have been mystified to find a key name absent from the index of a book before realising that there are two separate indexes – a subject index and an index of proper names. Some books even have a third index, of key passages cited from primary texts.

If you are writing an essay about slavery and the American Civil War, for instance, start by looking up 'slavery' in the index. If you are writing an essay about Stoic attitudes to the emotions, start with 'emotions'. This is blindingly obvious. However, if the first, obvious, item to look for is absent, don't give up. At this stage you need to start being more imaginative. Look for the names of key individuals: Chrisyppus or Cicero in the case of the essay on Stoicism. Or look up related themes or concepts: if there is no entry for 'emotions', try 'passions' or 'feelings' or even 'reason'.

In some cases, as in the example above of an essay about Christian responses to Darwin's theory of evolution in the nineteenth century, there is no obvious single term to look up in the index. There are lots of different things you can look up, based on the names and ideas that you have gleaned from your lectures. Imagine that the index contains the following entries:

creation, concepts of: 24, 57, 70, 73, 74, 76–7, 92, 127, 136, 141, 143, 146, 161, 162, 168, 175, 197, 210, 220, 232, 236, 237–8, 243, 246, 251, 271–2, 279–80, 281–3, 285, 293–4, 303–4, 305, 308, 311, 313–17

Darwin, Charles: 4, 14–15, 29, 31, 45, 47, 183, 197–8, 219–20, 221, 223, 224, 227, 242–3, 251, 253, 254, 255–63, 270–82, 292–3, 296–311, 313, 316–17, 324, 335

evolution; Charles Darwin's theory of: 4, 14–15, 16, 227, 231, 243, 247, 255–63, 274, 275–82, 321, 337–8

Huxley, Thomas: 5, 31, 36, 279, 281–3, 288–90, 305, 313, 321; debate with Wilberforce: 40–2, 49–50, 274

Kingsley, Charles: 293–4, 314

Temple, Frederick: 41, 274, 310, 317

theism; theistic evolution: 283, 303, 308, 311–17[4]

What you are looking for is *clusters* of pages, which, ideally, are referred to under more than one of the headings. As a rule of thumb, ignore single-page references (and those, like 76–7, which probably refer to a single paragraph that straddles two pages), and look only at references to a range of pages. Applying the rule in this case results in the following:

creation, concepts of: 281–3, 313–17

Darwin, Charles: 255–63, 270–82, 296–311

evolution; Charles Darwin's theory of: 255–63, 275–82

Huxley, Thomas: 281–3, 288–90; debate with Wilberforce: 40–2

theism; theistic evolution: 311–17

---

4 Taken from the index to John H. Brooke, *Science and Religion: Some Historical Perspectives* (Cambridge: Cambridge University Press, 1991).

You will then decide, on the basis of the questions that you have in mind as a result of thinking about the essay title, which of these clusters of pages to look at. The key section, in which the frequency of references is highest, will probably be, in this instance, pp. 270–317. So, by a quick look in the index, I would have found a section of under 50 pages to look through. Having skimmed that section, I might then find 10 or 20 pages of especially useful material. Using the index this way can save you hours of pointless grind. Once you have found the most important sections of reading material to look at, you can start taking some notes.

As well as making a note of the main clusters of pages to look at, it is worth noting down the first one or two references to a key topic or individual, even if they are isolated ones. Often that is where you will find introductory biographical information about an individual or a definition of a central concept. For instance, in the index of a book about the Stoic philosopher Epictetus, I find the following entry:

> emotions: 11, 27–8, 108, 114, 116, 133, 137–8, 146, 164–5, 178, 189–96, 209, 212–17, 244–54, 257–8

Clearly the main sections to look at will be pp. 189–96, 212–17 and 244–58. However, it might just be worth looking at the first entry or two as well. And, indeed, although the first one (on p. 11) is not particularly useful for my purposes, when I turn to pp. 27–8, I find an extremely useful definition:

> Following his Stoic authorities, Epictetus regards all mental states, including emotions, as conditioned by judgements. In desiring or in being averse to something, a person, according to this view, has formed a judgement concerning what it is good to pursue or bad to experience: emotions are the outcomes or concomitants of such judgements.[5]

First and last chapters, paragraphs, sentences

Sometimes, even after looking at the contents and the index, you may not have narrowed down the pages you have to read very

---

5 A. A. Long, *Epictetus: A Stoic and Socratic Guide to Life* (Oxford: Clarendon Press, 2002), p. 27.

significantly or helpfully. Now is the time to start *skim-reading*. This is a crucial academic skill. The introductions and conclusions to books are excellent places to start to find out what the basic thrust of a book is; what its general approach is; how it fits into the wider debate. Within chapters or articles, the first and last paragraphs can fulfil a similar function. Even within paragraphs, the first and last sentence can be all you need, as you skim through a few pages, to get the gist of what is going on. All you need to know at this stage is: 'Are these pages relevant to me for my current purposes, or not?'

As an example, let's suppose I am still working on the essay on Stoic attitudes to the emotions. I am now looking at one of the later ranges of pages in the book on Epictetus mentioned above, which look as if they will be relevant, and I am skimming through them as part of my survey of the material, looking just at the first sentence of each paragraph. I read the first sentence of the first new paragraph on the first page in the range I am interested in:

> Aristotle does not mean that everything human beings do is done of the basis of *prohairesis*.

That doesn't really sound relevant to Stoics and emotions to me. So I skip to the next one:

> The standard translation of Aristotelian *prohairesis* is choice, though 'decision' is sometimes adopted instead.

That's no better. What about the next one?

> It is unlikely that Epictetus studied Aristotle at first hand.

That's getting better – at least it mentions one Stoic. But I'm not really all that interested in the relationship between Epictetus and Aristotle at the moment. I want to get some basic information on what Stoics such as Epictetus thought about emotions. So I skip this one and press on to the start of the next paragraph:

> As a Stoic, Epictetus accepts the school's standard doctrine that the human mind is rational through and through.

Aha! That sounds more like it. So, I persevere with this paragraph. The next sentence is promising too:

In contrast with Plato and Aristotle, who divided the mind into rational and irrational faculties, he takes all desires and emotions to be true or false value judgements made by the mind as a whole.[6]

And, indeed, the rest of the paragraph and the next few pages all turn out to be on precisely the topic I am interested in: Stoic attitudes to passions and emotions. So I can make a note to myself that these are sections to come back to and take notes on.

First things first

The last thing to do before you actually start taking notes is to decide what order to read the material in. This is quite a simple process. The best policy will normally be to start with the most basic, general and introductory bits of reading and leave the more complex and detailed studies till last. You also need to think about when to read any primary material. You might prefer, in some cases, to read the primary material right at the outset, so that you can formulate your own response to it before reading what other people have argued. Or you might prefer to read it last of all, once you have all the alternative interpretations and arguments in mind, so that you can approach the primary material knowing exactly what sort of evidence would be most interesting, to confirm or disprove the leading theories. Once you have decided the order you will tackle the items on your list, you are ready to start reading and taking notes.

I have taken a whole chapter explaining the processes by which you get from looking at your reading list for the first time to the moment when you actually set pen to paper and start taking some notes. This may seem disproportionate, but these processes are such an important part of efficient and effective academic work, and can save you so many countless hours in the course of your degree, that they certainly merit their own chapter. Although I have devoted quite a lot of space to explaining these tasks, they are not in themselves very time-consuming. They will soon become second nature.

6 Long, *Epictetus*, pp. 212–13.

Chapter 5

Reading and taking notes

Summary

Read actively and selectively, not passively and indiscriminately. Avoid the mistake of copying out whole chunks of a book instead of making brief notes. Work out your own optimum note-taking strategy. Be on the look-out for particularly good quotations to use in your essay or presentation. If you have not understood or absorbed something, read it again. But learn when to cut your losses and move on if it really will not sink in.

Active reading

Before you start reading a text you need to know, as far as possible, what sort of text it is, who wrote it, when, why, and so on. The first thing to think about is whether it is a primary or a secondary text (on this distinction, see Chapter 2, pages 24–7). What are the main differences between reading primary texts and reading secondary texts?

Reading primary sources

If you are doing it right, it will take you longer to read primary texts than secondary ones. You can't really skim over primary materials in the way I described at the end of the last chapter in relation to secondary texts. When you pick up a primary text, which will most often have been produced in a distant time or place, you need to engage in an act of imagination – historical, transcultural, or both. When you read a text written by a Stoic philosopher, a Renaissance diplomat, or a nineteenth-century anti-evolutionist, you will get little out of it if you simply think to yourself that, according to your own present-day beliefs, this stuff is just wrong. You need to put aside your own preferences and prejudices. The failure to do so would result in a relatively uninteresting 'presentist' reading: a reading that is really a projection of your own views onto the text, or a refusal really to engage with the text because it does not fit with your own view of things. So, try not just to dismiss things by today's standards as racist, sexist, politically incorrect, or simply wrong. The fundamental point of reading primary texts is to understand what the text meant at the time and place of its production and reception. In the eyes of its producers and consumers (writers, publishers, printers, booksellers, readers), what was the text for? What did it achieve socially, politically and intellectually at the time? What mechanisms did the author use to try to bring this about? Why, for instance, did Machiavelli write *The Prince*? Who did he think would read it? What was he trying to persuade them to think or do? How did he hope it would reflect upon him? These are more historically pertinent questions than, for instance: Was Machiavelli right? Are human beings essentially manipulative? (The latter might, nonetheless, be good questions to have in mind if you were reading *The Prince* for a moral philosophy course rather than a history or literature course.)

Although you should approach primary texts sensitively and respectfully, you should not necessarily believe the accounts that they offer of the culture within which they were produced; nor what they have to say about other texts produced by their colleagues, rivals or enemies. All writing is propaganda. To take just one example, in her classic work, *The Second Sex*, first published in 1949, Simone de Beauvoir summarises all discussions of feminism produced during the preceding century as 'voluminous nonsense' that has done 'little to illuminate the problem'.[1] It is interesting that she says this, but not necessarily true.

The following checklist summarises some of the most fruitful questions to have in mind when reading a primary text:

✓ When and where was this text first produced?
✓ Who was the author?
✓ What do we know about them?
✓ How did they make their living?

1 Simone de Beauvoir, *The Second Sex*, translated by H. M. Parshley (London: Vintage, 1991), p. 13.

✓   What did they hope to gain by producing this text (fame, status, money, power, something else)?

✓   What literary, rhetorical or argumentative devices does the author use?

✓   Are they a reliable and accurate source?

✓   To what extent is this a piece of propaganda, and in service of what?

✓   Is this a conventional text or a convention-breaking one?

✓   Who is the author writing for; who is the target readership?

✓   Who actually did read the text?

✓   What would they have thought of it?

✓   Why is this text still read by academics and students today?

✓   Should it be?

Reading secondary sources

What about secondary sources? Normally these will have been produced quite recently and by people writing from within approximately the same cultural situation as yourself. When you pick up a secondary text, then, you can be in a slightly less respectful and empathetic, and a slightly more critical and argumentative frame of mind. Do not let yourself be convinced too easily. Be aware that what you are reading is someone else's opinions – informed and intelligent ones no doubt – but opinions all the same, not just a collection of objective facts. The writer of a secondary source has always selected which facts to present to you for a particular reason. Even historical accounts of events that seem pretty objective are opinionated and polemical to a greater or lesser extent. There is no single objective version of any historical event, nor any single correct reading of a text.

Also, be aware that we academics like to make our own views seem original and important by setting up a 'prevailing orthodoxy' from which we can then heroically dissent. Beware of this trick: it is rhetorically effective but not necessarily an accurate representation of the state of the field. As with primary texts, never forget when reading secondary texts that all writing is propaganda.

Taking notes

The basic technology

Until recently students and academics tended to make notes from books and articles in libraries using pen or pencil and paper. This is still a simple and easy option, but often nowadays using a laptop is also a possibility. If you are lucky enough to have a laptop at your disposal, there are a couple of things to bear in mind. First, you will need to check with the librarians in your library whether and where you are allowed to use your laptop, and whether you have to, for example, get it checked first, or use a special adaptor. Second, and very importantly, there is an additional danger when using a laptop to make notes, namely that you might accidentally cut and paste quotations from your reading into an essay without properly acknowledging them. This would constitute plagiarism, which is a very serious matter (for more on this, see Chapter 10, page 135). So it is particularly important to keep a clear record of what are your paraphrases of the texts, what are quotations from texts, and what are your own thoughts. In the example below, of some notes I took from a philosophy of science article about explanation, quotations from the article are within quotation marks, my own thoughts are within square brackets, and the rest is my paraphrase of the article:

p. 228
To explain empirical regularity you need to appeal to higher-order regularity . . . or explain in terms of a theory that suggests unseen *causes*

Such a theory: 'postulates entities, properties, processes, relations, themselves unobserved, that are held to be causally responsible for the empirical regularities explained'.

'This kind of explanation may be called *retroductive* because it leads backwards from the observed effect to postulated causes.'

[Hmm. Why not just say it is 'causal' or 'inductive' . . . ?]

'Retroduction' is Peirce's term – he also called it *abduction*

[Lipton says abduction = inference to the best explanation. Same thing as retroduction . . . ?][2]

---

2 Notes taken from Ernan McMullin, 'Two ideals of explanation in natural science', in P. Lipton (ed.), *Theory, Evidence and Explanation* (Aldershot: Dartmouth, 1995), pp. 223–38.

Take notes selectively but thoroughly

A very fast reader can read at a rate of one page every minute or two. No one can read and make good notes at that rate. I have explained in Chapter 4 how and why it is important to be selective about what to *read*. Equally, it is important to be selective about what, of the material you read, you *write down*.

People vary immensely in the way that they read, the way that they take notes, and the amount of noting that they do while they read. The amount of note-taking that people do when reading ranges from none (an almost universally disastrous strategy) to all; by 'all' I mean that their note-taking ends up consisting of just copying out the important paragraphs word for word. I have, at times, lapsed into the 'all' technique and so I know from experience that it is an immensely time-consuming and completely unsuccessful strategy (because one is simply postponing the essential task of actively *selecting* the most important material).

It will be for you to work out your own optimum strategy for note-taking. Most of the notes you take should be short paraphrases of what you are reading. Having decided that you need to note a section of a book, you should try to read one paragraph at a time and then note down a brief sentence or two summarising that paragraph. The notes need to be such that when you look at them months later (for instance, when revising for exams) they remind you what argument was being made, but they need not be in the form of full sentences, nor need they always be very detailed.

Bibliographic information

You should also always write down the author, title and date of the book or article you are noting (and, in the case of books, the publisher and place of publication too); and make a note of *which page* of the publication you are noting (whether for paraphrases or direct quotations) as you go along. All this information will be invaluable to you, both when you need to refer back to the original material, and when you need to provide footnotes and a bibliography for a formally assessed piece of work. Publication information will be available in the first couple of pages of the book. As an example, let's look at an edited book of essays on *King Lear*. Opening the book, we turn to the title page:

Critical Essays on
SHAKESPEARE'S
KING LEAR

edited by
Jay L. Halio

G. K. Hall & Co.
An Imprint of Simon & Schuster Macmillan
New York

Prentice Hall International
London   Mexico City   New Delhi   Singapore   Sydney   Toronto

So, the title and editor are clear. However, this page mentions three publishers and seven cities, but no date. In order to reduce this to one city, one publisher and a date, we turn over the page. There we find:

Copyright © 1996 by G. K. Hall & Co.

G. K. Hall & Co.
An Imprint of Simon & Schuster Macmillan
866 Third Avenue
New York, New York 10022

On the basis of this, we can now decide to give G. K. Hall, New York as the principal publisher, and 1996 as the date of publication.

Suppose that I am taking notes from the essay in this book by Alexander Leggatt. I would now be in a position to include full bibliographic information at the beginning of my notes (ready to use in the bibliography of my essay or dissertation – see the section on this at the end of Chapter 9, page 123):

Alexander Leggatt, 'Madness in *Hamlet, King Lear*, and Early Modern England', in Jay L. Halio (ed.), *Critical Essays on Shakespeare's* King Lear (New York: G. K. Hall & Co., 1996), pp. 122–38.

As a general rule, if there are several publishers and/or cities mentioned, use the first one in the list. If you are still not sure, you can use COPAC[3] or your own university library catalogue to see what decision librarians have made about what to include as the definitive publication information. (Conventions of referencing and bibliography are discussed more fully at the end of Chapter 9, pages 119–23.)

Paraphrases and quotations

Your account of the information and ideas you have learned through your reading should find its way into your essay in the form of an intelligent paraphrase, not a simple reproduction of someone else's words. A small amount of the material you read, however, will be so crucial to the essay you are about to write, or so well phrased, or perhaps so completely, even comically wrong that it will make an ideal quotation to use in your essay. So, when taking notes, be on the look-out for a handful of good quotations, always making sure you do not fall into the 'all' mode of note-taking, which is, in fact, just copying out whole paragraphs and pages from the book.

There is a difference between primary and secondary material when it comes to taking notes. As I have stressed several times already, primary material is the lifeblood of academic work in the arts, humanities and social sciences. Primary texts are your most important source of evidence. So, although the majority of secondary material you read can and should be paraphrased rather than quoted directly in your essay or presentation, you should expect to quote from primary sources quite frequently. You should read primary sources as carefully, rigorously and imaginatively as possible. Really think about how each phrase and each sentence could be interpreted. And think about which sections would, if quoted in your essay or presentation, have a particularly powerful impact in helping to make your case.

Collecting the evidence

The majority of the time available for each assessed written project or presentation you take on for your degree will be taken up with reading and making notes. It is important, therefore, that you make

3 See <www.copac.ac.uk>. For more on COPAC, see Chapter 6.

good use of that time from the outset. Keep reminding yourself to be active and selective. Imagine that you are a lawyer or an investigator collecting evidence to use when building a criminal prosecution to be presented in court. You need to accumulate a clear general picture of what happened (the general background to the question) and also collect 'killer' bits of evidence than clinch your case (key examples, quotations, facts). This way you should end up with an informative set of notes on a wide range of material – the ideal starting point for thinking about how to put your essay together.

Don't fall asleep!

Taking notes from books and articles, even when done actively and selectively as outlined in this chapter, can become a rather soporific process after a few hours. There is always the danger of falling asleep (mentally, physically, or both). So you need to develop strategies to avoid your brain switching off. The most obvious way is to give yourself regular breaks. Probably a 10-minute break per hour's work is about right. More than that can make a serious dent in the amount of actual work you get done, but less could result in boredom and lack of concentration. You will sometimes find that you are so engrossed in what you are doing that you don't need a break – in which case, lucky you!

Your *thoughts*, your *examples*

A very important technique to develop to keep yourself mentally and physically awake is to interject your own thoughts into your notes as you go along. This helps to keep a mental dialogue going between you and the author you are reading, rather than engaging in reading in a passive way. It also helps you to keep reminding yourself what the essay title you are working towards is, and to keep thinking about how the material you are reading and noting will be relevant. Taking notes, like reading, should not be a passive process. You should be actively analysing, examining, interrogating the text. This involves thinking, and writing down your thoughts, as well as reading and recording the content of the text.

Inserting your own comments in the midst of your notes is also a way to make connections with other things you have read for this or for other essays. You can interpolate comments such as 'See also Smith on Plato – this is the same argument', or 'Is this the same as

what Dr Noggins said? Check lecture notes', or 'This is rubbish –
use as example of misuse of Marxist theory'. The way that I have
always done this is to use square brackets to enclose the comments I
want to make myself, to distinguish them from notes and quotations
from the text I am reading (as in the example on page 62).

Inserting your own comments as you go along is a way of getting
your thoughts together in preparation for what you want to write in
your essay, presentation or dissertation. If you are really struck by
something you read, it might set off a whole chain of thoughts
(about how and why you agree or disagree; or about what this
section of a text demonstrates), which you should write down while
it is fresh in your mind. If you insert these sorts of reflections on
your reading while you are taking notes you are, in effect, already
starting to write your essay or presentation. You can then go back to
these thoughts later and refine and develop them for the final version
of the piece of work you are producing.

Finally, try to think of your own examples to illustrate or, just as
importantly, to contradict the argument or analysis that you are
reading and noting. If a philosopher says that explanations often
invoke causes, even if she provides some examples, try to think of
some more of your own, and some counter-examples. The same
would go for a literary critic claiming that a particular play is sexist:
try to think of cases that support this interpretation but also of parts
of the play which portray women in an affirmative and constructive
way. If a historian claims that a particular social struggle was an
instance of class conflict, make a note to yourself of what his evidence is, and then try to think of examples that undermine that
generalisation (upper-class individuals on the allegedly working-class
side of the divide, and vice versa).

Know when to move on

Sometimes when you are reading a primary or secondary text you
will hit a section that you really do not understand. In a primary
text, you might come across references to the science, philosophy,
medicine, religion or politics of a different time or place which it is
very difficult to understand without some more background knowledge. In either a primary or a secondary text you might come across
an argument which, even after reading it two or three times, you
cannot get to grips with. I have a vivid memory from my own
undergraduate days of reading Jean-Paul Sartre's *Being and Nothingness*.

I reached a paragraph that, as I recall, was explaining the difference between two different kinds of being; or it might have been two different sorts of nothingness; or it might have been two different sorts of 'and', for that matter. In any case, it made not the slightest bit of sense to me. But I was a conscientious student, so I read it again. It made even less sense the second time. So I calmly read it again. No improvement. So I went down to the kitchen and made a cup of tea. Then I came back up to read it for a third time. After which I calmly threw the book across the room before deciding to move onto the next paragraph and give up on that one. I had a similar experience with something by Heidegger, too.

It is important to stretch yourself and to make a real effort to understand the texts you have been asked to read. Nonetheless, when you are reading and taking notes, one important skill to develop is recognising when it is time to move on. As I have repeatedly emphasised, your time is your most valuable resource, and you must make the best use of it. Re-rereading paragraphs you don't understand by Sartre and Heidegger (for instance) can be a little like banging your head against a brick wall. You would do much better to make a note to yourself to ask your lecturer to explain the sections you did not understand at a later date, and to spend the time making notes on, and thinking about, the sections you have managed to get to grips with already.

Academic Latin

Another potential obstacle to easy comprehension of academic texts is the habit academics have of lapsing into Latin or other foreign languages (including academic jargon that is purportedly in English) from time to time. In the case of academic jargon you should probably have a dictionary handy, or use the internet to decipher unfamiliar terms. Academics do not use Latin as much as they used to, but in case you do come across Latin terms or abbreviations which mean nothing to you, I have provided a short list below of some of the most commonly used ones, and their meanings. I will come back to some of these (namely *e.g.*, *i.e.*, *ibid.* and *op. cit.*) in Chapter 9, pages 109 and 120.

You may find that some of these (such as *et al.* and *ibid.*) are quite useful shorthand with no obvious, established English equivalent. However, I would not encourage you to get into the habit of using many of the others. I think that including Latin phrases and abbreviations is one of the best ways to make your writing less accessible. As a rule, you should try to think of an elegant, plain English alternative. I include the following list of terms, then, primarily to help you decipher the writing of those who do not apply this principle, and not as an encouragement to use them yourself.[4]

AD   Short for *Anno Domini*, meaning 'the year of our Lord'. The Western calendar traditionally starts from the (supposed) year of the birth of Jesus Christ. This Christianised convention of giving years as 'AD' or 'BC' (the latter standing for the English phrase 'before Christ') is gradually falling into disuse. Many people nowadays prefer to use more neutral and inclusive abbreviations. 'AD' is then replaced with 'CE' (standing for 'common era') and 'BC' is replaced with 'BCE' ('before common era').

ad absurdum   As in the phrase *reductio ad absurdum*; a term used to describe a way of ridiculing an argument by showing that it has absurd consequences when taken to its limit.

ad hoc   For this particular purpose.

ad hominem   Literally, 'to the man'; the feminine equivalent is *ad feminam*; these terms are used to describe rhetorical attacks that are aimed at the individual rather than their argument. In football parlance, making an *ad hominem* argument could be described as 'playing the man instead of the ball'.

ad infinitum   To infinity; without limit; endlessly.

ad nauseam   To an excessive or disgusting degree.

a posteriori   Literally, 'from what comes after'; a term used in philosophy to mean reasoning or knowledge that comes after observation or experience, in contrast to *a priori* reasoning or knowledge.

a priori   Literally, 'from what comes before'; a term used in philosophy to mean a form of deductive reasoning or knowledge not dependent on observation or experience; used more generally, with more negative

---

4 In compiling this list I have made use of Eugene Ehrlich, Nil Desperandum: *A Dictionary of Latin Tags and Phrases* (London: Hale, 1985).

	connotations, to mean an opinion or conjecture not tested by evidence or critical examination.
c. or *ca.*	Short for *circa*, meaning 'about'; as in 'The industrial revolution has traditionally been dated to the period *c.*1750–1850' or 'This piece of sculpture dates from *ca.* 400 BCE'.
cf.	Short for the Latin (rather than the English) word *confer*, meaning 'compare'. This abbreviation is sometimes used in footnotes to indicate that the argument being offered compares in interesting ways with another account published elsewhere, as in: '*Cf.* Biggins (2002) for an alternative version of events.'
Cogito ergo sum	Descartes' famous maxim, meaning 'I think, therefore I am'. This tends to be quoted in Latin; it is sometimes referred to simply as Descartes' '*cogito*'.
de facto	In reality; in fact.
de jure	By right; according to law.
e.g.	Short for *exempli gratia*, meaning 'for example', as in 'Some people, e.g. Michel Foucault, have argued that knowledge is simply a form of power'.
ergo	Therefore.
et al.	Short for *et alii, et aliae* or *et alia* (masculine, feminine and neuter, respectively), meaning 'and others'. You are most likely to come across this abbreviation in reading lists or bibliographies, as a way to indicate that a book or article has several authors, only the first of whom has been named, as in: 'John W. Boyer *et al.* (eds), *Nineteenth-Century Europe: Liberalism and its Critics* (Chicago: University of Chicago Press, 1998)'.
etc.	Short for *et cetera*, meaning 'and so on', 'and the rest', or 'and others'.
ex cathedra	Literally, 'from the chair'; a phrase meaning 'with authority', derived from the practice of a pope pronouncing infallibly from his papal throne; sometimes applied to academic experts making authoritative pronouncements.
ex nihilo	Out of nothing; as in 'creation *ex nihilo*'.
explanandum	That which needs explaining.
explanans	That which does the explaining; explanation.

fl.	Short for *floruit*; literally, 'he or she flourished'. This is used to indicate the period in which a writer, artist or composer was working actively, especially when exact dates of birth and death are not known; as in: 'The frescoes in the Certosa of Pavia are by the Italian painter, Bergognone, also known as Ambrogio Stefani da Fossano (*fl.* 1450–1523)'.
ibid.	Short for *ibidem*, meaning 'in the same place'; used in footnotes or references to refer to the work cited in the immediately preceding footnote or reference.
i.e.	Short for *id est*, meaning 'that is', as in 'The most influential French thinker of the twentieth century – i.e. Jacques Derrida – is now widely taught in both philosophy and literature departments'. I.e. can be replaced with 'that is to say' or 'in other words'.
inter alia	Amongst other things.
NB	Short for *nota bene*, meaning 'note well' or 'take particular notice of the following'.
non sequitur	Literally, 'it does not follow'; used to refer to a conclusion or argument that does not follow from what has gone before, even though it is presented as if it does.
op. cit.	Short for *opere citato*, meaning 'in the work cited'; used in footnotes or references to refer to a work cited earlier.
pace	Literally 'peace'; used to mean something like 'with all due respect to', when disagreeing with someone, as in: 'I will argue below, *pace* Hume, that much human knowledge is based on *a priori* judgements'.
per impossibile	Although it is impossible; which could not be true; as in: 'supposing, *per impossibile*, that you witnessed a cat metamorphosing into a hamster'.
per se	Intrinsically; in itself.
QED	Short for *quod erat demonstrandum*, meaning 'which was to be demonstrated'. 'QED' is written at the end of mathematical proofs to indicate that the author has now proved the thing they set out to demonstrate.
qua	In the capacity of, or in the role of; as in: 'Browning, *qua* poet, has no explicit political message'.

q.v.	Short for *quod vide*, meaning 'which see'; sometimes used to cross-reference entries in encyclopaedias and other works of reference.
sic	Thus; so. This word is often used, within square brackets, to indicate that a mistake or misspelling in a quotation was in the original source. In the following example, it is an errant apostrophe that the author wishes to distance himself from: 'As Thomas Jefferson wrote to a friend in 1793, most in America at this time were "friends to the constitution" and anxious to "have it administered according to it's [*sic*] own republican principles."'
sine qua non	Literally, 'without which not'; an indispensable pre-condition.
status quo	The way things are; the prevailing state of affairs.
sui generis	Literally, 'of its own kind'; meaning one of a kind or totally distinctive.
vice versa	Literally, 'the change being turned'; conversely; the other way around.

As a general rule, Latin (and all foreign-language) phrases and abbreviations should go in italics. However, some have become such a familiar part of English usage that writers might judge that they do not need to be italicised. Examples from the above list, which might quite often not be italicised include 'ad hoc', 'ad nauseam', 'a priori', 'etc.' and 'vice versa'.

That's enough Latin for the moment. Let me round off this chapter by offering you a checklist of the main points covered above – the key things to remember about active and selective reading and note-taking:

✓ Work out how much time you have available.
✓ Calculate how many pages of each book/article you have time for.
✓ Be sure not to spend time reading irrelevant material.
✓ Check in the index for the key topics you need to know about.
✓ Avoid copying out large chunks instead of making brief notes.
✓ Keep a look-out for particularly good quotes.
✓ Think about both the big picture and also key bits of evidence.
✓ Think of yourself as a lawyer collecting evidence for a case.
✓ Make a note of the author, title, date, and publisher of each book you use.

✓ Keep a note of page numbers as you go along.
✓ Distinguish between notes and quotations.
✓ Distinguish between notes of what you've read and your own thoughts.
✓ Know when to move on.
✓ Have a dictionary handy.

Chapter 6

Using the internet

Summary

Be selective and discriminating. Only rely on sites run by competent and reputable individuals and organisations. Often these sites will be run by academic departments. But sometimes magazines, newspapers, broadcasters, museums and others produce the most authoritative and useful online information. Start from recognised 'hubs'. Make use of online texts. Ask lecturers and librarians for guidance.

What a load of rubbish!

The main problem with using the internet for academic research is that the huge majority of the material posted on the internet is complete garbage. Aside from the endless pornography, there are all sorts of ludicrous sites run by cranks and lunatics, as well as those set up by well-meaning but ill-informed enthusiasts on various individuals and subjects. You will also be able to find bad undergraduate essays generously posted on the web for you to consult. Almost everywhere you look, it seems, you are confronted with wall-to-wall rubbish.

Where to start

You should not despair, however, of finding useful and reliable information on the internet. There are increasing numbers of really excellent educational and academic sites available, from historical time-lines and encyclopaedias to online versions of literary texts. Once you have found the right sites, you will find that the internet is a wonderfully quick and easy source of information. It is a particularly good place to look for general overviews and introductions to topics, as well as for basic facts, dates, and so on, and for some primary texts. For more sophisticated discussions and interpretations, however, it is still best to rely on academic books and articles, which are guaranteed to have been properly 'peer reviewed' prior to publication (that is to say, they will have been read and appraised by other academic experts in the field).

As ever, the key is to be selective. An essay or presentation that makes good use of authoritative websites as sources of information, images and primary and secondary texts, can be outstandingly good. An essay or presentation that makes use of the first vaguely relevant site that came up on a quick search, regardless of its credentials, can be ghastly.

Ask for guidance first

Much the quickest way to find the most relevant and reliable websites for your subject is to ask the lecturers and librarians in your department or university. They will be able to tell you the best places to start and to introduce you to the electronic and online resources that your department and university subscribe to. You will be able to save huge amounts of time by having access to online biographical, bibliographical and other resources.

Five academic uses for the internet

The following five tasks are amongst those that can be most profitably undertaken with help from the internet:

- Finding *dates* of key individuals, events and publications
- Getting basic *background* information about a topic
- Discovering *biographical* information about an individual
- *Bibliography*: identifying the main academic books and articles on your topic
- Getting access to primary and secondary *online texts*.

Let's look at each of them briefly in turn as a way to illustrate some of the reliable and helpful resources to be found on the internet.

(One task that the internet can be used for that I am not discussing
in this chapter is looking for images; this is particularly useful when
giving a presentation, so I discuss it in Chapter 8.)

Finding dates of key individuals, events and publications

Imagine that you have been asked to write an essay about the French
Revolution and are confused about the basic dates and order of events.
You know that the key year is 1789, but you have also come across
references to the Revolution covering a five-year period from 1789
to 1794; and to something called the 'Terror' which seems not to be
quite the same as the Revolution proper. You decide that before
you even start trying to track down items on the reading list, you
need to be clear in your mind about this basic chronology and
wonder if the internet will be able to help. Your lecturer has recommended a site called 'Internet modern history sourcebook: French
Revolution', which is where you start.[1] It certainly seems very useful:
it contains links to summaries of key events and also to primary texts.
From this page you are able to work out that there was something
called the 'liberal revolution' of 1789–1791, followed by the 'radical
revolution' from 1792 onwards. Still wondering about the significance of 1794 and the 'Terror', you search the page for the word
'terror' (by pressing Ctrl-F, and then typing the word 'terror' into
the 'Find' dialogue box that appears). Doing this leads you to a link
to another page on the site. You click on that link and are taken to
a page which starts as follows:

Maximilien Robespierre: Justification of the Use of Terror

Maximilien Robespierre (1758–1794) was the leader of the
[twelve-man] *Committee of Public Safety* elected by the National
Convention, and which effectively governed France at the
height of the radical phase of the revolution. He had once
been a fairly straightforward liberal thinker – reputedly he slept
with a copy of Rousseau's *Social Contract* at his side. But his
own purity of belief led him to impatience with others.

---

1 <http://www.fordham.edu/halsall/mod/modsbook13.html> (accessed 19 January
2004).

The committee was among the most creative executive bodies ever seen – and rapidly put into effect policies which stabilized the French economy and began the formation of the very successful French army. It also directed [its] energies against counter-revolutionary uprisings, especially in the south and west of France. In doing so it unleashed the *reign of terror*. Here Robespierre, in his speech of February 5, 1794, from which excerpts are given here, discussed this issue. The figures behind this speech indicate that in the five months from September, 1793, to February 5, 1794, the revolutionary tribunal in Paris convicted and executed 238 men and 31 women and acquitted 190 persons, and that on February 5 there were 5,434 individuals in the prisons in Paris awaiting trial.

Robespierre was frustrated with the progress of the revolution. After issuing threats to the National Convention, he himself was arrested in July 1794. He tried to shoot himself but missed, and spent his last few hours with his jaw hanging off. He was guillotined, as a victim of the terror, on July 28, 1794.[2]

The rest of the page is taken up with excerpts from Robespierre's speech of 5 February 1794. So, now you are ready to move on to some further reading, knowing not only that the Revolution tends to be divided into 'liberal' and 'radical' phases, but also that the significance of 1794 was that this was the year that saw the execution of the architect of the 'reign of terror', then at its height, Robespierre himself.

Getting basic background information about a topic

You have been asked to prepare a presentation on the topic of 'conflict theories of crime and deviance' for a sociology class. You have been to the library and looked at a couple of textbooks, and have still not really worked out what conflict theories of crime and deviance actually are. You have e-mailed your lecturer to ask her for guidance, but it turns out that she's away for the rest of the week, so you decide to try your luck with the internet. You start with a couple

2 <http://www.fordham.edu/halsall/mod/robespierre-terror.html> (accessed 19 January 2004).

of general sociology sites recommended to you by your lecturer at the beginning of the year. These don't seem to have anything about conflict theory and crime, so you resort to using Google. You type into Google:

> sociology "conflict theory" crime

(The point of the quotation marks around "conflict theory" is to make sure that the sites you are offered contain that exact phrase.) The first site Google comes up with is a site hosted by the University of Missouri, St Louis. Specifically, it is a set of notes provided by a sociology instructor at that university on the subject of 'culture conflict theory'.[3] You gather from a quick read of this page that conflict theorists understand the definition and labelling of certain behaviours as 'crimes' as one of the many symptoms of conflict between dominant and minority cultures in society; more powerful groups try to impose their norms on less powerful groups whose interests are in conflict with theirs. The site picks out Thorsten Sellin, George Vold and Austin Turk as important conflict theorists of crime and deviance, and provides a short reading list. You note down the names of the books (none of which were on your original reading list) and prepare to head back to the library.

Discovering biographical information about an individual

When writing essays or dissertations you should always identify anyone whose words or ideas you want to use but who you had not heard of before, whose name you may have come across in a secondary source. (Of course, if you want to refer to someone as famous as Shakespeare, Plato, Abraham Lincoln or David Beckham, you need not supply any additional identifying information; it would be redundant to refer to 'the famous Greek philosopher, Plato' or 'the English footballer, David Beckham'.) If you cannot find an explanation of who the person is in the secondary source that names or quotes them, then the internet is likely to be able to provide you with the information you need. Let me offer a couple of examples.

---

3   <http://www.umsl.edu/~rkeel/200/culflic.html> (accessed 8 January 2004).

Suppose you are writing an essay about Darwinism and Christianity in the nineteenth century and you come across a reference to Asa Gray as someone who tried to reconcile Darwinian science and Presbyterian faith. You decide you want to mention her as an example in your essay. So, you write the following sentence:

> **Many in America also struggled with Darwin's theory, including a certain Asa Gray, who tried to combine belief in evolution with her Presbyterian faith.**

It is a busy week, and you also have a deadline for an essay about women's suffrage in Britain. You have come across a couple of references to a writer called Ray Strachey. Apparently he was one of the first historians of the Victorian women's movement. You decide you should mention him, even though you don't know anything about him, so you take a stab at writing something plausible:

> **The academic Ray Strachey, for example, produced his early history of the women's movement in the 1920s. It is still one of the most reliable accounts of the movement.**

But then you think: Perhaps I should find out a few more facts before finalising my essays. So, you go to Google and type in "Asa Gray" (within double quotation marks so as to search only for the exact phrase 'Asa Gray' rather than any page that happens to contain both the words 'Asa' and 'Gray'). The first website that comes up in the list of results is a page called 'Lefalophodon: An informal history of evolutionary biology web site'. Reading the first sentence of this page you discover that Asa Gray (1810–1888) was 'America's leading botanist in the mid-19th century'. The description continues: 'Darwin's strongest early supporter in the U.S., in 1857 he became only the third scientist to be told of his theory (after Hooker and Lyell).'[4] Aha – '*he*'!

Then you try the same for 'Ray Strachey'. The first item that Google suggests this time is an entry for a site called 'AIM25: Archives in London and the M25 area'. The page you are directed to is an entry for the 'Strachey papers', held at the Women's Library

---

4 <http://www.nceas.ucsb.edu/~alroy/lefa/Gray.html> (accessed 7 January 2004).

at London Metropolitan University. Searching for the name 'Ray Strachey' you find, at the bottom of the page, a reference to 'Strachey, Rachel (1887–1940), suffragist and author (as Ray Strachey)'.[5] Grateful for this new information about the sexes and occupations of Asa Gray and Ray Strachey, you can amend your essays:

> Many in America also struggled with Darwin's theory, including the leading botanist Asa Gray, who tried to combine belief in evolution with his Presbyterian faith.

> The suffragist and writer Ray (or Rachel) Strachey, for example, produced her early history of the women's movement in the 1920s. It is still one of the most reliable accounts of the movement.

Bibliography: identifying the main academic books and articles on your topic

Your lecturers will provide you with reading lists for any assessed project they have set you. However, the items on this list might not be available, so one of the ways you might use your initiative and go beyond the reading list is to use the internet to search for other texts to read. There are at least three different approaches you could take to this. You could look for online reading lists provided by other lecturers at your own university or elsewhere. Secondly, you could use an online library catalogue such as COPAC to look for books on your subject (see the example I gave of searching for books on women's suffrage in Chapter 4, pages 45–50). You can use COPAC as a rough and ready guide to what are the most widely used standard secondary texts on a given subject. Suppose you are writing a dissertation on Simone de Beauvoir and the construction of gender. As a starting point you might want to look at recent books on the subject. So, as a preliminary step, you might go to COPAC, choose 'Author/Title Search' and in the 'Title' field (rather than the 'Author' field, since what we want is books *about* Beauvoir, not books *by* her), type 'Simone de Beauvoir'.[6] On this occasion, that search produces 578 results, which seems rather excessive, so you decide to go back

---

5 <http://www.aim25.ac.uk/cgi-bin/search2?coll_id=6756&inst_id=65> (accessed 7 January 2004).

6 <http://www.copac.ac.uk> (accessed 19 January 2004).

and limit the search to books published since 1990. You do this by typing '1990-' in the 'Date published' field. This produces 113 results, which you then sort into reverse date order, so that you can see the most recent first. The most recent book is the *Cambridge Companion to Beauvoir*, published in 2003.[7] This is, at the time of your search, held by 13 of the 24 libraries searched by COPAC, which indicates it is widely considered to be a useful book on Beauvoir. Scanning through the list will reveal several more books that fall into this category, which will be useful starting points for your preliminary survey of Beauvoir scholarship. So, you can use COPAC as a sort of crude popularity contest – if lots of libraries have a particular book, all else being equal, it is more likely than not to be an important and useful one.

How about identifying relevant recent journal articles? This is something on which it will be best to consult with your lecturers and librarians, in order to find out which online journals and databases your institution subscribes to. One of the most useful online resources (and one of the most widely subscribed to amongst UK universities) is JSTOR: 'The scholarly journal archive'.[8] JSTOR offers you the facility to search every word of the text of articles from leading journals in a wide range of disciplines going back, in some cases, over a century. It is incredibly useful. Suppose that you are now at a slightly more advanced stage of your research into Simone de Beauvoir and the construction of gender. You log onto the JSTOR search page and enter the following search:

"gender"	in *full text*	AND
"construction"	in *full text*	AND
"Beauvoir"	in *title*	

From the range of different disciplines on offer, you ask JSTOR to perform this search on journals in history, language and literature, and philosophy. The search produces the following four articles:

Margaret A. Simons
'Sexism and the philosophical canon: On reading Beauvoir's *The Second Sex*' (in Reviews)

---

7 Claudia Card (ed.), *The Cambridge Companion to Simone de Beauvoir* (Cambridge: Cambridge University Press, 2003).
8 <http://uk.jstor.org> (accessed 19 January 2004).

Journal of the History of Ideas, Vol. 51, No. 3. (Jul.–Sep., 1990), pp. 487–504.

Judith Butler
'Sex and gender in Simone de Beauvoir's *Second Sex*'
Yale French Studies, No. 72, *Simone de Beauvoir: Witness to a Century*. (1986), pp. 35–49.

Virginia M. Fichera
'Simone de Beauvoir and "The Woman Question": *Les bouches inutiles*'
Yale French Studies, No. 72, *Simone de Beauvoir: Witness to a Century*. (1986), pp. 50–64.

Elaine Marks
'Transgressing the (in)cont(in)ent boundaries: The body in decline (in Beauvoir and Sartre)'
Yale French Studies, No. 72, *Simone de Beauvoir: Witness to a Century*. (1986), pp. 180–200.

Not only does this identify four articles for you to seek out and read for your dissertation, but it also identifies an entire issue of a journal devoted to Beauvoir, namely *Yale French Studies* **72** (1986). Because this is JSTOR, it also offers you instant online access to the articles themselves and the option to print them out too, which brings me onto the fifth and final academic use of the internet I want to mention: accessing texts online.

Getting access to primary and secondary online texts

The number of primary and secondary texts that are now available online, one way or another, is increasingly exponentially. There are online journals and archives such as JSTOR (and many others). There are e-books available to download (and pay for) and electronic libraries to which your university may or may not subscribe. Most widely available are online versions of classic texts (which are no longer protected by copyright). These come in all sorts of different editions – some more useful than others. One of the main hubs for online books is the 'Online Books Page' hosted by the University of Pennsylvania, which offers free access to over 20,000 books.[9] Let's take as an example Charles Darwin's book *On the Origin of Species*, first published in 1859. The Online Books Page offers links to six different online versions of this classic work. The most useful turns out to be the one hosted at a site devoted to 'The Writings of Charles Darwin on the Web'.[10] Why is this one the most useful? Because it is the only one which provides the text of the different editions of the work as they originally appeared. In effect this site gives you access to the original nineteenth-century texts and the ability to compare the successive editions, and to quote from them as if from the originals.

And finally...

As I have said, the place to start, when thinking about which websites to use for your studies, is not this book, but the advice of your lecturers and librarians. However, let me finish by mentioning one very useful and reliable hub for sites in a range of disciplines, namely the British Academy's PORTAL website. This is a site that I often use myself as a starting point when wanting to get quick access to reliable information on a subject I know nothing about. The homepage of the site is self-explanatory:

> Welcome to PORTAL, the British Academy's directory of online resources in the humanities and social sciences. It is designed as an entry point to available resources for those working in higher education and research. It covers:
>
> * Classical Antiquity
> * Theology and Religious Studies
> * African and Oriental Studies
> * Linguistics and Philology
> * Early Modern Languages and Literature
> * Modern Languages, Literatures, and Other Media
> * Archaeology
> * Medieval Studies: History and Literature
> * Early Modern History to *c.*1800

---

9 <http://digital.library.upenn.edu/books> (accessed 19 January 2004).
10 <http://pages.britishlibrary.net/charles.darwin> (accessed 19 January 2004).

- Modern History from *c*.1800
- History of Art and Music
- Philosophy
- Law
- Economics and Economic History
- Social Anthropology and Geography
- Sociology, Demography and Social Statistics
- Political Studies: Political Theory, Government and International Relations
- Psychology[11]

And don't forget that you can also visit www.getafirst.com for more useful tips and links.

---

11 <http://www.britac.ac.uk/portal> (accessed 19 January 2004).

Chapter 7

Planning an essay, presentation or dissertation

Summary

After you have finished reading and researching and before you start writing there is a crucial intervening step – thinking. This is the most important stage of all: the stage that determines whether your essay, presentation or dissertation will be likely to get a first-class mark. Think about your title. What are the key words? What are the hidden assumptions? Why is the topic controversial? Why is it interesting? What is your answer to the question? Talk your thoughts over with a friend. Then write a brief plan. Different people find different ways of planning better. But not having any plan is worst of all. This thinking and planning stage is the key to producing a really good essay or presentation rather than a merely competent one.

After reading and before writing: thinking

Whether you are preparing a presentation, an essay or a dissertation, it is crucial that before you start writing it, you know what you are going to say. It is also important that what you are going to say is interesting and intelligent, which is why you need to think carefully and creatively and draw up a plan of what you are going to say. Most of what I say in this chapter is based on the assumption that you are producing a plan for a piece of written work rather than a presentation. Very similar skills are required for planning a presentation. I will mention some differences in Chapter 8.

For most of my own undergraduate career I laboured under the misapprehension that what I was required to do when producing an essay was to read some books and then write an essay based on what I had read. This view of the task was not inaccurate, but it was incomplete. The crucial step that I had been missing out was the *thinking* step. In my third year a supervisor pointed this out to me. He suggested that after finishing my reading and noting I should spend some time, perhaps half an hour, or perhaps more, just thinking about the question I had been set and how I was going to answer it. My supervisor suggested to me that while doing this I indulge whatever was my favourite vice – in his case it was eating biscuits. Some other vices would be less appropriate accompaniments to this thinking stage.

Clearing your mind

Your hours of reading and note-taking are over. You have all the evidence and your thoughts about it written down (or printed out) in front of you, and some of the books themselves sitting next to you. What now? How to turn these into an essay or presentation? The best thing you could do at this stage is pick up all your notes and books and go and put them in a different room, or lock them away in a cupboard. You don't need them for the moment. Having completed your reading and note-taking you are now an expert on the subject. What you need now is a clear mind and some distance from the nitty-gritty of the material in order to think about the central argument you are going to make in your essay or presentation.

Brainstorming

Don't expect to come up with a brilliant argument straight away. Nor should you just sit there passively and wait for inspiration to strike as if you were a romantic genius of some sort. Thinking is an active process. A good way to encourage yourself to start developing some interesting ideas is to 'brainstorm' for a few minutes. Get a piece of paper and write down, first, the essay title, and then all the most important points you might want to make and the crucial bits of evidence. At this stage they don't need to be in any particular order, but you might start putting asterisks next to really important ones and question marks next to more dubious ones, and so on, just to get a preliminary picture of the key themes and examples. The following is the result of some preliminary brainstorming for an essay about George Eliot:

Could George Eliot's *Middlemarch* be described as a manifesto for altruism?
Who is the altruist? Dorothea? George Eliot?
*Religion of Humanity
*Morality without Christianity
*Eliot – intellectual background – Herbert Spencer, G. H. Lewes
*Difference between self-sacrifice and self-effacement
*Is altruism a fundamentally self-centred characteristic in Dorothea?
****SYMPATHY is the key – feelings and attitudes rather than altruistic actions
Self-effacement and objectivity (Levine)??
Victorian context – 1870s – urban poor??
****Can a novel be a 'manifesto'?

Talk to a friend (real or imaginary)

Once you've done some initial brainstorming, instead of continuing to sit alone munching chocolate digestives and mulling over your thoughts, an even better idea is to discuss the topic with a friend. Hopefully you will find that one of your friends is prepared to talk with you about altruism in George Eliot, or the invention of the Renaissance, or the conflict theory of crime, or the construction of gender, or whatever. You will be able to reciprocate when they come to write their next essay. Having a conversation with someone about the questions you are thinking about is by far the quickest and best way to do your thinking. It is no coincidence that from Plato's writings onwards, philosophers have always favoured the dialogue as one of the best genres for philosophical investigation. Conversations accelerate your analysis better than anything else. Having to express in plain conversational sentences what you are thinking and how you are planning to argue for your view is an excellent preparation for writing the essay. If you can't find a willing friend at the appropriate time then use your imagination – talk to a chair and imagine it is occupied by an intelligent person who is basically ignorant of your subject, and then spend half an hour discussing your essay with them.

An essay is an argument

Fundamentally, an essay is an argument – it is an extended written argument, which brings evidence and reasoning to bear in an attempt to persuade the reader. (A presentation is, similarly, an attempt to persuade an audience.) If the essay title you have been set is a good one, it is very likely to make reference (implicitly or explicitly) to an ongoing academic dispute about how to interpret a certain culture, period, literary corpus, individual philosopher, or historical event. You are being invited to join in this academic argument, and the most engaging way to do so is by developing your own argument about the best way to interpret the disputed topic.

Again, it is useful to think of yourself as a lawyer in court – an advocate of a particular case, marshalling relevant evidence to persuade a neutral panel of reasonable people of your point of view. There are, of course, different sorts of essays: some essay titles encourage you to take a stance, others seem to be asking for more of a balanced discussion. But even essay titles that end with the instruction 'Discuss' are asking for an argument rather than for a book report or a shopping list. It is never a good idea just to produce a meandering review of your reading, nor a shopping list of different facts and different opinions vaguely related to the theme of the essay. You do, of course, need to get a certain amount of information across – you cannot persuade your reader without appraising them of relevant information along the way – and you also should show that you have understood the reading you have done. Your first priority, however, and the task that should motivate everything that you write in the essay and the way that you structure it, is the job of arguing your case. By way of illustration, below are some examples of different essay titles and the cases you might have decided to argue (labelled A for analytical and argumentative) and also, in each case, a less analytical, more discursive approach (labelled D for discursive), which would be less likely to result in a first-class essay.

Title: **Could George Eliot's *Middlemarch* be described as a manifesto for altruism?**

A: Critics have often described *Middlemarch* as being based on an 'altruistic' ideology. Eliot's own language, however, refers to a 'wider sympathy', which is subtly different from the idea of 'altruism'. Sympathy is a sort of inward mental attitude, altruism a sort of self-sacrificing, charitable action. In this essay

I explain why it would be better to describe *Middlemarch* as a manifesto for feelings of sympathy than for altruistic actions.

D: *Middlemarch* promotes altruism in three ways: through self-sacrificing romantic relationships; through ideas about charity and philanthropy; and through Dorothea's own religious feelings. So, I will discuss how *Middlemarch* certainly could be described as a novel that promotes altruism. On the other hand, in each case, there are ways that the narrator seems to approve of a certain level of selfishness. I will also discuss these before providing a conclusion.

Title: **Simone de Beauvoir famously wrote, in *The Second Sex*, 'one is not born a woman, but becomes one'. Discuss.**

A: Beauvoir's *The Second Sex*, despite its huge initial public popularity, has been neglected by feminist writers who feel that, in her enthusiasm to deny sex differences, she became too enamoured of the ideals of maleness. In this essay I will explain why Beauvoir's *Second Sex* is, in fact, a refreshing antidote to much recent feminist writing on sex and gender. Beauvoir's famous saying that 'one is not born a woman, but becomes one' is still particularly relevant in the face of modern scientific attempts (by proponents of evolutionary psychology) to reduce gender differences to sex differences.

D: Simone de Beauvoir was a great feminist writer who was very popular in her time. Most people nowadays think that her writings are somewhat *passé*, however. She denied that men and women were fundamentally different. Feminists these days reject Beauvoir's views, although sometimes seeing merit in them still. I will discuss whether *The Second Sex* is still a classic of feminism or if it should, on the other hand, be consigned to the dustbin of failed theories. I will conclude that although Beauvoir's views were important in some ways, in others they have been superseded.

Title: **How do sociologists use conflict theory to explain crime and deviance?**

A: To answer this question, we need to be a little more specific. There are different kinds of conflict theory and different kinds of crime and deviance. Generally speaking, conflict theorists interpret crime and deviance as concepts deployed by more powerful social groups to repress less powerful ones. However, as I will argue below, this is more persuasive in some cases than others. In the case of a social group, such as a teenage peer group, it is clear that a dominant sub-group can exercise control over a perceived deviant using positive and negative sanctions. Such a simple model is not so easily applied to criminal law in a democratic society, however. I will conclude that, in these more complex cases, conflict theory is totally inadequate.

D: Sociologists use conflict theory to show how the rich and powerful in society repress the poor and powerless by inventing concepts such as crime. There is no such thing as right and wrong, fundamentally, but only what society decides to impose on people for its own reasons. In this essay I will give examples of how crime and deviance are used to repress minorities in various different ways, as suggested by conflict theorists who look at class conflict and race conflict in society, and some examples of why people have criticised this.

You will notice that one of the differences between an analytical, argumentative essay and a less interesting, discursive one is that the former often points out an important distinction that the essay title is in danger of overlooking, while the latter simply produces a rather general response to the title. First-class essays tend to be argumentative; to pay rigorous analytical attention to the essay title; and to make distinctions rather than working with generalisations. I will come back to this last point in the section in Chapter 10 entitled 'Make distinctions', pages 129–30.

Do you need to be even-handed?

One of the most common misconceptions about academic essays is that they should always be balanced and even-handed. There is some truth behind the misconception. You must always show that you are aware of the evidence and arguments deployed by those authorities you are arguing against in your essay. And you should give a fair and accurate account of those views, rather than setting up a weak or exaggerated version of their views that is very easy to knock down – a 'straw man'. However, you do *not* have to defend all sides of the argument, nor give a totally even-handed account of each side.

If you look back at the examples of more discursive and less analytical arguments given above, these tended to employ a boringly even-handed sort of approach. Argumentative essays, presentations and dissertations are more engaging and interesting to read than directionless discursive ones, but strong argumentation should always go along with a clear understanding of the views being argued both for and against. Generally speaking, the best argumentative essays will highlight both the strongest and the weakest parts of an opposing case. The strongest parts should be analysed, taken apart and challenged with good evidence. The weakest parts can be mentioned simply as a rhetorical device to undermine the credibility of an opposing case. Some polite and gentle mockery or ridicule may be in order. Often, however, a weak argument can be left to speak for itself.

What's your point?

You should be able to summarise the point of your essay in a short sentence or two. If you cannot manage this then you probably don't yet have a clear argument. Ask yourself questions like 'What is my basic point in this essay?', 'What am I trying to show?', 'What is the key idea I want a reader of this essay to take away from it?'. The examples above of essay titles and possible arguments provide an idea of the sort of thing you are looking for.

Writing your plan

Essays and presentations that have been planned are better than those that have not been planned. It is as simple as that. You should plan presentations and essays both for assessed work and in exams. It only takes a few minutes. The first and last sections are always the same: 'Introduction' and 'Conclusion'. The intervening sections (normally a smallish number of them, in the region of three to five, depending on the length of the presentation or essay) should be arranged in a logical order so that your argument unfolds smoothly and clearly. It should always be clear when you are moving from one section to the next, and how and why you are doing so.

Different people construct plans in different ways. Being a very prosaic and unimaginative person myself, I have always favoured linear plans that simply break the argument down into constituent parts and then arrange them in order. However, more creative people tell me that they prefer to use 'spider diagrams' or 'mind maps', which allow for more unexpected connections to be made between different clusters of ideas and themes. You can experiment and see what works for you. The most important thing is to make sure you leave some time for this process – a sort of organised brainstorming – so that you can successfully map out the shape of the argument and evidence of your essay.

Throughout the reading, note-taking and thinking process, you will have been focusing on the title and thinking about the analysis and examples you need in order to produce a convincing argument. If you broke the title down into sub-questions, as I suggested in Chapter 4, in order to clarify what you needed to look for in your reading, then that will be helpful too when drawing up the plan. Be realistic about how much you can say in the time or number of words available to you. Keep it simple. The end result will be something like the example below.

Could George Eliot's *Middlemarch* be described as a manifesto for altruism?

1. Introduction: Can a novel be a manifesto?
2. Origins of term 'altruism'
    a. Auguste Comte and the religion of humanity
    b. Eliot's friendship with Herbert Spencer
3. Dorothea the altruist
    a. Romantic altruism – example
    b. Philanthropic altruism – example
4. BUT 'altruism' not the same as sympathy
    a. Feelings or actions?
    b. Eliot's own language: 'wider sympathy' – examples
5. Conclusion: If a manifesto, then for sympathy, not altruism

How to use your notes

At various points both before and after the planning process you will need to read through your notes. Once you have made your essay plan, you might find it useful to go back through your notes and mark the particularly important parts in the margin with the number of the section in your essay to which they will be relevant. Or you could use colour coding, making a different coloured mark in the margin of your notes to indicate the different theme or section of your essay to which they relate.

Speaking more generally, while you are planning your essay and while you are writing it, you need to decide how much use to make of the notes you have made from your reading. I suggested above that, when clearing your mind for the initial process of thinking and brainstorming, you should put your notes and books away out of sight. You might want to go even further and write the first draft of your essay with your notes still locked away out of sight. This may sound daunting, but it is actually surprisingly easy – especially if you have been through the processes of active reading, thinking, talking through and planning suggested above. You just need to write a succinct paragraph or two to explain what each point on your plan means. When you have done this you will find that you have written a first draft of your essay. This technique has enormous benefits in terms of producing a lucid, readable and argument-driven piece of work rather than something that resembles a shopping list or a mishmash of unconnected, cut-and-pasted thoughts and quotations. Another great advantage of writing a first draft in this way is that you will inevitably produce your own paraphrase of other people's arguments rather than succumbing to the temptation to rely too heavily on quotations or to use the author's own words in a barely changed version.

Another useful technique you could employ at this stage in the planning/writing process is – once you have worked out what your argument is going to be – to start off by writing the *conclusion* to the essay. This is a good way to focus your mind on what the rest of the essay is working towards.

However far you get with your books and notes locked away, you will, at some stage before producing the final version of your essay, need to consult them again; at this stage you can pick out particularly useful quotations and examples with which to illustrate your arguments. You can also make sure at this stage that there aren't any crucial things in your notes that you have forgotten about, and that you have represented other people's views fairly and accurately.

Chapter 8

Giving a presentation

Summary

It is very likely that in the course of your degree you will be required to give at least one presentation, which may or may not be formally assessed. Some people find this a particularly daunting prospect. It need not be. The same reading, thinking and planning skills that can be used when writing an essay can also be used when preparing a presentation, but with some important differences. Think about how to keep your audience engaged by using pictures, props, videos and PowerPoint presentations. Have a clear 'take-home message'. Produce a handout. Engage your audience. Giving a presentation is not the same as reading an essay aloud.

Use your fear

According to Social Anxiety UK, an organisation for sufferers of social phobia, the fear of public speaking is one of the most common of all fears, not only among individuals with social phobia, but for everyone.[1] However, fear of public speaking certainly need not be pathological. It is perfectly natural to feel some apprehension. As an academic, my job involves a lot of public speaking: giving lectures, running seminars, and delivering papers at academic conferences.

---

1 Social Anxiety UK: <http://cgi.social-anxiety.org.uk/research/prevalence.htm> (accessed 20 January 2004).

And I still get nervous, especially when speaking to an unfamiliar audience or on a topic I have not spoken about in public before. It is natural to be worried, since I care about what the audience thinks of my presentation. If they are students I am concerned that the lecture should be clear and helpful. If they are other academics at a conference, I am anxious that they should find my research interesting.

The emotion of fear serves a useful purpose. It alerts you to an imminent danger and prepares you physically and mentally to respond to it. In the case of an assessed presentation, your fear (although hopefully you won't have *too* much) should motivate you to prepare well in order to minimise the risk of things going badly on the day. When it comes to actually delivering the presentation, a modicum of fear will provide you with that edge of nervousness and adrenalin, which will help you perform well. In my experience, the time to be really worried about how a presentation is going to go is when you *don't* feel nervous.

This chapter offers some tips on how to minimise the fear you feel when it comes to delivering your presentation. Some people recommend breathing exercises. Other people say you should try to imagine everyone in the audience naked in order to defuse your fear. I have never tried this, but can only think it would be dreadfully off-putting. The advice I offer in this chapter is to minimise the anxiety you feel on the day by using your fear to motivate you to prepare thoroughly in advance.

As with so many aspects of academic life, preparation is absolutely critical. Whether or not you write a good essay is very much dependent on whether you made efficient use of your time when reading and taking notes, and whether you spent enough time on the thinking and planning stage. Similarly, with a presentation, how well it goes is largely determined by what you do before you step into the room. If you are well prepared – if you have done your research, constructed your argument, thought about how to hold your audience's attention, and got hold of images and other props to illustrate your case – you will have nothing to fear.

(Before moving on, I should say that I do not at all intend to dismiss the fear of public speaking as trivial or easily conquered simply by thorough preparation. If you find public speaking genuinely distressing, then that it something that you will need to address with your lecturer or tutor. However, I am afraid that it is not something that I can deal with this within the remit of this book.)

A presentation is a performance

When preparing a presentation you will need to use many of the same reading, thinking, planning and writing skills that you would use when preparing to write an essay or dissertation. However, there are several differences, which are what this chapter is about. These all arise from the fact that a presentation is a performance – a bit of theatre. You have many more techniques at your disposal than you do when writing an essay. Giving a presentation is not the same as simply reading an essay aloud! If you want to get a first-class mark for your presentation, the following are the things you need to think about.

(In what follows, I am talking primarily about assessed presentations. More informal and non-assessed presentations in seminars and classes are also important opportunities to develop your skills and understanding. These were discussed in Chapter 3.)

Researching

You need to be every bit as rigorous in your reading and researching for a presentation as for an essay or dissertation. In order to give a persuasive presentation you need to be in command of the primary and secondary material as much as you do when producing a written piece of work. There are one or two additional considerations, however, that will give your research a slightly different slant.

First of all, you should be on the look out for any good visual aids right from the outset. The internet can be useful for this. Suppose that you are giving a presentation on the themes of blindness and madness in *King Lear*. You remember your lecturer mentioning that the eighteenth-century English artist George Romney had produced some famous illustrations of Shakespeare's plays, including *King Lear*. A quick search brings up the website of the Folger Shakespeare Library in Washington DC, which includes a page of Romney's drawings with some accompanying information, produced in connection with an exhibition of Romney's work a few years ago.[2] One of these is a very evocative picture of Lear himself, which might make a powerful image to include in a presentation either as a sort of

2 <http://www.folger.edu/public/exhibit/Romney/Romney.htm>   (accessed   21
   January 2004).

backdrop or to illustrate a particular point. Many websites on classic texts and important historical figures and events have sections specifically devoted to images. Make the most of these.

The internet is certainly not the only place to find visual aids for your presentation. You can also be old-fashioned about it and look in books, both in the library and in bookshops. Think about what would be a particularly useful image. What would help illustrate the point you want to make about the period, text or event in question? Might a contemporary painting, or a political cartoon, or the frontispiece of a famous book, or an image of an artefact or piece of material culture be most effective? Try not to use images just for the sake of it. Although a photograph or painting of someone might help to give a human face to a name and thus bring your argument to life a little more for your audience, there are also many more interesting uses to be made of images. You can also think about making your own visual aids. Perhaps a table or diagram, or even a PowerPoint presentation that you have produced yourself might be the best way to illustrate the point you want to make.

And you don't have to stop at still images – think about using moving ones too. In the case of *King Lear*, for instance, there are several film versions available. You could watch one or more of these and think about how the direction, lighting or sound are used to enhance the themes you are interested in of blindness and madness. You could even think about comparing these treatments with another famous film treatment of a mad monarch – *The Madness of King George*, based on Alan Bennett's play, *The Madness of George III*. Are there any particularly striking, short clips from any of these films that you could use to illustrate your talk?

It is not only presentations on literary or theatrical topics that could benefit from the use of film clips. Many historical, philosophical, theological and scientific themes are treated in films. A presentation about the French Revolution could make use of clips from the film version of Dickens's *Tale of Two Cities*. A presentation about medieval theological disputes might be brought to life with clips from *The Name of the Rose*. However, as with still images, do not use film clips just for the sake of it. As with quotations and examples in essays, visual aids in presentations must always be motivated and justified by the thrust of your argument. You will get no credit (from your lecturer at least) for a crowd-pleasing string of clips from movies if they do not help you to make an interesting argument about the topic of the presentation.

In Chapter 10, I discuss the most effective ways to begin and to end an essay or dissertation. Beginnings and endings of presentations are also critical. The two things that an audience remember most in any talk are the first thing you say and the last thing you say. You can allow yourself a little more theatricality and rhetorical bravado in a presentation than in an essay – it is a performance, after all. This means that you should be on the look-out, when you are doing your reading, for particularly striking quotations with which to open or close your presentation. If you are giving a presentation about the causes of the American Civil War, and arguing that, contrary to the views of some revisionist historians, the issue of slavery was absolutely fundamental to the outbreak of the war, it might be effective to end with a quotation from one of the leading protagonists which makes this issue central – a quotation from Jefferson Davis's farewell speech to the US Senate in January 1861, for instance. Confronting your audience with primary evidence like this can have a powerful effect.

Whether using your own words, or a decisive quotation from a primary source, the beginning and the ending of your presentation should be designed to have a direct, powerful and memorable impact.

Thinking

When you are reading a piece of academic writing, if you come to a sentence or paragraph that is particularly difficult or important, you can slow down, pause, think about it, read it again, pause again, think about it again and then carry on. When you are listening to an oral presentation, you can't do that. For your presentation to be effective, therefore, it has to be clear what you are saying at the first time of asking. I am not suggesting that it is all right for your written work not to be clear. I think you should aspire to clarity in that, too. However, there is perhaps more room for complexity in an essay or dissertation than in a presentation. This does not mean that your argument in an oral presentation cannot be original, sophisticated or unexpected. It should be all those things. But it should not be convoluted or over-complex. Your points need to be both sophisticated and clear, both transparent and innovative. This is the ideal to have in mind at the thinking and planning stage.

In practice, this means that you should have a clear 'take-home message' and no more than two or three points. It also means that you should, out of consideration to your audience, regularly flag up how far through the argument you are, how many points have been covered, how many are still to come, and so on. You can also help your audience by providing a handout, like a lecture handout, which indicates the structure of your talk and, perhaps, includes some crucial quotations, names, dates and images.

One of the best things a presentation can make people in the audience think to themselves is: 'Hmm. That's interesting. I'd never thought of it like that before.' It is at the planning stage that you can think about how to elicit that reaction. Try to think laterally. For instance, in the case of a presentation about madness in *King Lear*, imagine that you read an essay on madness in Lear that argues that *Lear* offers a particularly realistic representation of the experience of madness in the period.[3] This might start you wondering how to find out more about the real experiences of madmen and madwomen in early seventeenth-century England. What were the theories of madness used by physicians or priests? What was the relationship between medical and religious practice? Can you find any books about the history of psychiatry that might be relevant? Did physicians of the time believe there was a link between physical blindness and madness, or perhaps the reverse? Were there cases of blind people with accentuated sensory and mental powers of other kinds? Can you find any pictures from the period (in books, or on the internet) of what a madhouse would have been like? An audience expecting a presentation primarily about textual interpretation would have their attention fixed quite effectively by an unexpected tack such as this one.

Another way to keep your audience on their toes is to keep the conclusion of your argument under wraps until the last minute, or to include in your conclusion an unexpected twist, a killer piece of evidence, or a sudden resolution of the problem you have been discussing. However, you should only do this if you are sure you have the evidence and arguments to back it up. Again, you should not try to be theatrical just for the sake of it.

In summary, when planning the structure of your presentation, think about your audience. Will they follow it? Will it be interesting for them? How will you set it up with a narrative structure that will

---

3 Alexander Leggatt, 'Madness in *Hamlet, King Lear*, and early modern England', in Jay L. Halio (ed.), *Critical Essays on Shakespeare's* King Lear (New York: G. K. Hall & Co., 1996), pp. 122–38.

keep their attention? How can you present the problem and the evidence in an engaging way? How can you clearly explain the controversy you are talking about and persuade them round to your point of view? Given the limitations of time and complexity that a presentation format imposes, what are the most important parts of the argument and the very best pieces of evidence? Those will be all you have time for.

Communicating

What I have been saying so far in this chapter, about researching and thinking, has all been based on the important fact that a presentation is a performance and not just an essay. You need to think about how to communicate your ideas effectively to an audience. This applies most directly of all when it comes to the stage of composing and then delivering the presentation.

The first question to ask yourself is how much material you can cover in the time allocated. Let's imagine you have been asked to give a 30-minute presentation. Do you know how many words you can say, at a reasonable pace, in that time? You should time yourself to find out. For most people the figure will be between about 125 and 175 words per minute. Let's say you decide that you speak at about 150 words per minute, when speaking at a moderate pace that can easily be followed by an audience. That means that in 30 minutes you could say around 4,500 words. However, there are several reasons why you should not aim to produce a script for yourself that is, in effect, a 4,500-word essay.

First of all, you should probably not be aiming to produce a script in any case. It is very hard to keep the attention of your audience and get them to feel engaged if you are just reading out a script. Working from notes will be more effective. Secondly, even if you were preparing a script for yourself, it would not be much like an academic essay. It would need to be written in a style more like the one I have adopted in this book – a somewhat more informal, chatty and direct style (while still, hopefully, not sacrificing precision). While writing this book, I have often been imagining myself actually saying what I am writing, in the way that I would if you were sitting here in my office and I were offering you my thoughts on study skills face-to-face. When writing a talk, you should do the same thing. Try to hear yourself saying the words. Thirdly, you need to leave time for pauses and for any other business that will take up time, such as taking transparencies on and off an overhead projector, or switching a video or DVD on and off.

People differ in the way that they prepare presentations. What I have often done is to write a talk of approximately the length required (in this example, about 4,500 words), and then to go through and replace each paragraph with a one-sentence note-form summary, just as a reminder of the theme. When doing that, I would, of course, leave any quotations I wanted to use there in their entirety, along with important dates, names and book titles that I wanted to be sure to get exactly right.

It is, in one way, much more reassuring to have a script in front of you. But it is just so difficult to deliver a script in a lively and engaging way, you would do much better to resist the temptation by not even taking a script in with you. You don't need a script when someone asks you about what you've been doing recently, or about your job, or your relationship, or your hobby, or your academic work, for that matter. Why not? Because these are all things you know and care about and have clear opinions about, which you can articulate spontaneously. If you are well prepared for your presentation, the same will be true for the topic of your presentation. It will be something you know and care about; you will know, without a script, what you want to persuade your audience of and what the key facts are that will support your case. If you wanted to persuade someone to share a house with you, or set up in business with you, or to lend you a large amount of money, you would think in advance about how to go about persuading them, but would not expect to succeed if you took a script along with you and read it out to them. The same is true of any presentation. Spontaneous human speech has a directness and persuasiveness that not even the best script can emulate.

If the problem with having a script is that you will seem inhuman, rigid, detached, even boring, the problem with using notes is that – if you are anything like me – you will be in danger of going on and on, and of wandering off in whatever direction your mind takes you, and of ending up covering only about a quarter of your points, and then suddenly realising that your time is up. The best way to avoid this is to practise your talk a few times in advance to get a sense for how much time you have for each point and when you need to move on. You could write at the top of each page of notes an approximate time at which you need to move on to the next page.

When it finally comes to delivering your presentation you will probably be nervous. As I said at the outset, this is absolutely natural and, within reason, a good thing. If you are well prepared and well practiced you have nothing really to worry about. Try to relax and imagine you are just talking to a group of friends and trying to persuade them of something important. Hopefully that won't be far from the truth. Being relaxed in this way does not mean being sloppy and imprecise in the way you express yourself, or delivering an unstructured talk, or making lots of jokes, or using slang. It means delivering your clearly structured talk in a natural and direct manner, even if you are feeling tense and nervous inside.

There are whole books written about public speaking, which go into detail about different techniques for dealing with nerves, and different ways to engage your audience and keep their attention (I recommend one of these books in the further reading section at the end of this book). I think that the most important thing is to be well prepared, and there is not much more advice I want to offer you about delivery than to try to be natural, relaxed, direct and persuasive.

There are, however, just three specific things that I want to mention about the actual delivery of your presentation. First, make sure you have some water available. Speaking for 20 or 30 minutes will give you a dry mouth whether you are nervous or not. It is also quite helpful for you and the audience to take a pause every now and then during your talk – drinking some water is a helpful visual cue for such a pause.

Second, make eye contact, especially, but not exclusively, with whoever is assessing the presentation. Eye contact is fundamental to human communication. What I try to do when giving a presentation is make eye contact with as many different people as possible. Let your eyes wander round the audience, stopping here and there for some eye contact as you go.

Third, you need to think about gestures and body language. You should make use of these: they are valuable communicative tools. Think about when a forceful hand gesture might help to reinforce your point. Something that I often try to do is to use body language to reinforce visually a distinction I am making in the talk or lecture. Sometimes I do this by walking a couple of paces away from the lectern to make the first point, and then walking back to where I was to deliver the contrasting point. Something else you could try is physically placing different examples and arguments using your hands.

I do this by making a gesture as if I were putting something down on a table in front of me. You can line two or three of these up in their imaginary places in front of you and then gesture towards them as you go through them in turn. You can watch your lecturers, politicians, TV presenters and the like to see how they use body language, effectively or not. Don't overdo it, though. Excessive gesturing and moving about, or nervous fiddling with hair, paper, pen, or water bottle can be distracting and annoying.

Try to enjoy the performance, and don't lose sight of the fact that, for all the emphasis I have placed in this chapter on the performance side of presentations, the fundamental task at hand is the same as for written academic work: you are trying to persuade an intelligent audience, in clear and precise language, of your point of view on an interesting and contentious topic, using logic, evidence and rhetoric.

Chapter 9

Writing essays and dissertations I
The basics

Summary

One thing which is guaranteed to annoy your lecturers and to cost you marks in assessed work and exams is a tendency to make basic errors of spelling, punctuation and grammar. Try to eliminate such errors from your writing. This chapter includes a list of particularly common mistakes made in student essays, which should be avoided at all costs. It also explains the basics of referencing and bibliography. Always read your work through before you hand it in!

The basics

You may find the advice contained in this chapter rather patronising or unnecessary. Perhaps, for you, it is unnecessary. But then again, perhaps it isn't. All the advice contained in these sections is simply accumulated from comments that I have regularly needed to make when marking undergraduate essays.

Handwriting and spelling

Examiners are only human; maybe they shouldn't give very much weight to things such as handwriting and spelling, but I can tell you from experience that marking an essay that is difficult to read because of the handwriting, or which contains a lot of basic errors of spelling or grammar that need correcting, is a wearisome and unpleasant experience. Wearisome and unpleasant experiences put people in bad moods. And people in bad moods give essays lower marks than people in good moods do.

You can do yourself a big favour by making sure that you have learned to write legibly, spell correctly and use grammar properly by the time you take your exams. Your aim should be to make no spelling or grammatical mistakes in assessed essays or in exams. Every such mistake is unnecessary and can be eliminated by a careful read-through of your essay. (Although, being realistic, we all miss some mistakes even after reading a piece of work through several times, and so one or two undetected slips will not count against you – I expect there are a handful in this book despite the best efforts of myself and the copyeditor.)

Most of the rest of this chapter consists of a list of some of the most common mistakes made in student essays and an explanation of correct usage. At the end of the chapter I will also give an overview of the proper use of two important academic tools: the footnote and the bibliography.

Some common mistakes corrected

The following list of mistakes includes errors of spelling, punctuation and grammar. Common problems with structure, argumentation and style will be covered in the next chapter. Once you have read the next few pages, you will know your affects from your effects, your colons from your semicolons, and your principals from your principles. You will know how to use pronouns and prepositions, what constitutes a sentence, what a split infinitive is, and how to use 'literally' correctly. In other words, you will know how to avoid getting on the wrong side of pedantic lecturers like me!

Affect and effect

'Affect' is normally used as a verb. To 'affect' something means to alter or influence it:

> The relationship between science and religion in the nineteenth century was affected [altered or influenced] by the professionalisation of science.

When it is used as a noun, 'affect' means feeling or emotion.

'Effect' is normally used as a noun. The 'effect' of something is its impact, outcome or result:

One of the effects [results or outcomes] of the professionalisation of science in the nineteenth century was a transformation of the relationship between science and religion.

'Effects' can also mean property; someone's 'effects' are their belongings. When it is used as a verb, 'to effect' something means to bring something about, as in the following phrase: 'The police officer effected an arrest.'

And and but

Some people will tell you that it is incorrect to start a sentence with 'and' or 'but'. But, in fact, many of the best writers start sentences that way from time to time; it can be an effective way to give a point rhetorical force. And you should experiment with it yourself. But you should not overdo it. And be warned that some lecturers might not like it.

Apostrophes

An apostrophe indicates one of two things:

- A missing letter
- Possession

'It's raining' and 'Don't do that' are examples of apostrophes indicating missing letters. Other examples are 'they're', 'who's' and 'you're' (see below). 'Smith's argument' and 'Price's dog' are examples of possessive apostrophes.

'Its' (meaning 'of it') is an exception; even though it is a possessive pronoun made by adding an 's', it does not have an apostrophe. This is simply to distinguish 'its' (meaning 'of it') from 'it's' (meaning 'it is'). The following example shows the correct usage of both: 'It's easy to remember when to use an apostrophe; its use is relatively straightforward.'

When using an apostrophe to indicate possession, and the word or name already ends in 's' (perhaps because it is a plural) there are two equally acceptable alternatives: either put just an apostrophe after the final 's', or add an apostrophe and another 's'. So, 'the argument of Dickens' becomes either 'Dickens' argument' or 'Dickens's argument', and 'the advice of Thomas' becomes either 'Thomas' advice' or 'Thomas's advice'.

Potentially confusing cases occur when a plural word does not end in 's': common examples of this include 'children' and 'people'. In these cases, the apostrophe should come before the 's', since it is a possessive 's' and not a pluralising 's': hence 'the children's toys', 'the people's princess'.

What an apostrophe does not indicate is that a word is in the plural. When making a plural, you never use an apostrophe. The plural of 'banana' is 'bananas', not 'banana's'.

Beg the question

A lot of people misuse the expression 'begs the question'. It does not mean 'demands that the following question be asked'. To beg the question is to provide a supposed answer to a question that, in fact, covertly assumes the truth of the answer rather than providing an argument for it. In other words, to beg the question is to give a circular argument – an argument that tacitly includes the conclusion amongst its premises. Imagine that you asked me whether politicians can generally be relied upon to tell the truth and I replied, 'Certainly they can. Why, I heard Tony Blair just the other day saying that he and all the other members of the cabinet always tell the truth!' I could then be said to be begging the question. This is because one of the hidden premises of my argument was that Tony Blair (a politician) was telling the truth when he said that he and his cabinet colleagues were truthful people. In other words, I was covertly just assuming the truth of the proposition for which I was supposed to be providing a justification.

Colons and semicolons

There is only one piece of punctuation misused more frequently than the colon and the semicolon: the apostrophe.[1] A colon is used as a prelude to a list, quotation, or new piece of information. A colon means something like 'here it comes'.

1 For an excellent book on punctuation, which is both informative and entertaining, see Lynne Truss, *Eats, Shoots & Leaves* (London, Profile Books, 2003).

A semicolon is like a big comma; it indicates a major pause or break in the sentence; it is mid-way in strength between a full stop and a comma. The separate parts of a sentence separated by one or more semicolons should normally be able to stand as sentences in their own right; they are separated by semicolons rather than full stops as an indication that they are concerned with the same theme or event or idea as each other. In summary, they separate a sentence into sub-sentences. In a sentence separated into two parts by a semi-colon, the two parts should somehow illuminate each other; the second part might, for instance, narrow the scope of a general state-ment made in the first part.

Commas

Commas are used to separate items on a list, or to help a reader through a long sentence by implying pauses. They can also be used in pairs, as in this sentence, to separate off a parenthetical comment. A common misuse of the comma is to insert it before 'however' or 'nevertheless':

> General de Gaulle refused to compromise, however his opponents would not be intimidated.

Here the two parts of the sentence should be separated by a semi-colon and a comma could be added after 'however':

> General de Gaulle refused to compromise; however, his opponents would not be intimidated.

Although a comma should not be used before 'however' or 'never-theless', it is often helpful to use one before other conjunctions, such as 'and' and 'but':

> General de Gaulle refused to compromise, but his opponents would not be intimidated.

> General de Gaulle refused to compromise, and his opponents grew heartily sick of it.

The correct or incorrect use of commas can make a real difference to the meaning of a sentence. You should take care to use them correctly.

The following is just one example of the different meanings a sentence can have, depending on the presence or absence of commas:[2]

> I like some chilled drinking water at lunchtime.

> I, like some, chilled, drinking water at lunchtime.

Criterion and criteria

A criterion is a principle, standard, or test by which a thing is judged, assessed, or identified, or by which it is included or excluded from a given category:

> The primary criterion for categorising an author as 'postmodern' is their rejection of all master-narratives.

The plural of criterion is criteria:

> There are several criteria by which academic excellence might be judged: erudition, strength of argument, writing style, or originality.

e.g. and i.e.

Avoid using these abbreviations if at all possible! There are plain English alternatives which make for much more attractive prose. If you are not sure what they mean, see the section on 'Academic Latin' in Chapter 5, pages 68–72.

Foreign-language phrases

Latin (and other foreign-language) phrases should go in italics (or be underlined if you are writing by hand).

He, she, they

This is not so much a common mistake as a stylistic conundrum. In cases where you are referring to an individual who could be male or

---

2 For more examples of the ways that punctuation can dramatically alter the meanings of sentences, see Truss, *Eats, Shoots & Leaves*, pp. 8–13.

female, and subsequently want to refer to that individual with a pronoun, you need to decide which pronoun to use. The same problem arises when wanting a pronoun to stand for 'anyone' or 'everyone'. The options include 'he', 'she' and 'they'. An alternative term, which has been invented specifically to deal with this problem, is 's/he' or '(s)he'. When it comes to possessive pronouns, this last option does not work; the best you can do, if wanting to follow this inclusive approach, is to use 'his/her' or 'her/his' or spell it out fully as 'her or his'.

> Your lecturer will give you a reading list for each essay; *he* might place an asterisk next to the important items.
>
> Each student has to decide how *she* is going to spend *her* time at university.
>
> Each academic will have a different view about sentences. *They* might favour short, punchy sentences, or *their* taste might be for long, involved ones.
>
> How is a voter to react to such intimidation? Should *(s)he* simply capitulate?
>
> A philosopher's greatest asset is *his/her* time.
>
> The phrase 'secondary deviance' refers to the process by which the individual comes to identify *herself or himself* as deviant.

Each of the options is unattractive. The convention until quite recently was to use 'he'. This sexist usage does not have very many defenders today (although, surprisingly, I have encountered more than one female student wishing to hold on to the convention and resisting my suggestion that they replace 'he' and 'his' with something more inclusive). Some favour using 'she' and 'her' in all cases, as a sort of positive discrimination or affirmative action, counteracting centuries of bias in the other direction; others resist this reverse sexism. Using a plural pronoun ('they' or 'their') to replace a singular subject (such as 'each academic' in the example above) is taken by some to be the correct convention. But I have to say that for pedants like me this lack of agreement between subject and pronoun seems simply ungrammatical and, consequently, causes a certain amount of anxiety. Finally, '(s)he' and 'his/her' or 'her or his' are cumbersome and ugly. Which path you decide to follow, then, will depend upon whether you think it is worse for your prose to be characterised by anti-female sexism, by anti-male sexism, by grammatical incorrectness, or by downright ugliness. The compromise that I favour myself is to alternate between male and female. So, if a few pages back I called an imagined philosopher 'she', I will call the imaginary student I am writing about 'he', and make a mental note that the next imagined character of indeterminate sex should be female. (I have to confess that, as the eagle-eyed reader of this book will discover, I also sometimes grudgingly use 'they', when it seems to sound natural.) Everyone must decide for themselves how to solve this stylistic conundrum.[3]

Hyphens

Should phrases such as 'working-class' and 'fifteenth-century' be hyphenated or not? The answer is that it depends on whether the phrase is being used adjectivally or not. When it is being used adjectivally to describe, say, an event, text, movement or person, it has a hyphen; if it is being used on its own with the definite article, there is no hyphen:

This is a fifteenth-century painting, produced in Renaissance Italy.

Suffragism was not initially a working-class movement.

The Renaissance in Italy began in the fifteenth century.

Few suffragists in this period were from the working class.

Its and it's

See the section on apostrophes, above.

Literally

'Literally' is one of the most frequently and comically misused of words. To say that something is 'literally' the case is to imply that although the phrase being qualified by the word 'literally' may sound

3 For a novelistic account of an argument about the use of 'his', 'his or her' and 'their', see Julian Barnes, *Talking it Over* (London: Cape, 1991), Chapter 1.

metaphorical or figurative, you mean it to be taken in its most straightforward, non-metaphorical sense. For extra force, people often insert the word 'quite' before 'literally'. The following are examples of correct usage:

> While I was frying my breakfast at the campsite, I noticed a spider in the pan, which I quickly ejected with my spoon. That poor creature, quite literally, went out of the frying pan and into the fire.

> There were six of us in the kitchen trying to make some vegetable soup – all throwing in different ingredients. The resulting concoction was a repulsive sort of gruel. It was literally a case of too many cooks having spoilt the broth.

So much for correct uses of 'literally'. What about the comic and frequent misuses? I think that what people often mean when they use 'literally' inappropriately is something like 'really' or 'in all seriousness'. It is best, however, to reserve 'literally' for differentiating between figurative and non-figurative meanings. Otherwise you can end up with uses like the following which imply quite unlikely scenarios.

> I was so angry that I literally exploded.

> You might say that these exams aren't important; but if I don't do well, I will be, quite literally, gutted.

> Descartes was, quite literally, the father of modern philosophy.

> Simone de Beauvoir, for 1960s feminists, was literally the bee's knees.

'On behalf of' and 'On the part of'

'On behalf of' means instead of, in the place of, for, or as a representative or agent of:

> The Professor welcomed the undergraduate students on behalf of [as a representative or agent of] the whole department.

'On the part of' means of, by, produced by, or exhibited by:

> It was a great show, and it was a particularly impressive performance on the part of [by] Millicent Mildew.

This argument displays a tendency on the part of [of] Hume towards an empiricist understanding of the world.

That was very aggressive behaviour on the part of [exhibited by] John.

Phenomenon and phenomena

A phenomenon is a fact, process or event. More specific meanings include a very remarkable event, occurrence or person, or (in a philosophical context) a fact given by sense experience. The plural of phenomenon is phenomena. The following are examples of correct usage:

Sociologists and anthropologists are well aware of the phenomenon [fact] that religious rituals of one kind or another are found in all cultures.

Arsenal's success is a footballing phenomenon [remarkable event].

Young Margaret was fascinated by all kinds of political phenomena [processes and events].

The purpose of scientific theories is to explain the phenomena [facts given by sense experience].

Prepositions at the ends of sentences

Some people still insist that a sentence must never end with a preposition (such as 'with' or 'to'). I do not think you need to worry about this. In the section on 'Pronouns' below, I use a sentence ending in a preposition: 'In the examples below, there is ambiguity about what the pronouns (in italics) are referring to.' To avoid ending the sentence with 'to' I should perhaps have written: 'In the examples below, there is ambiguity about to what the pronouns (in italics) are referring.' This illustrates how following the rule that a sentence must never end with a preposition can give rise to very convoluted constructions. This is what Winston Churchill had in mind when he (allegedly) described the rule as 'the kind of arrant pedantry up with which I will not put'.

Principal and principle

'Principal', when used as an adjective means 'leading' or 'most important'. 'Principal' can also be used as a noun, as in the principal of a school or college. 'Principle' is only ever used as a noun, as in the phrase 'on principle' or 'the principles of mathematics'. A principle is a fundamental truth, rule, code of conduct, or axiom.

> She was the principal at the local school, and the principal bread-winner; she refused, on principle, to share her income with her husband, who was writing a book on the principles of economics.

Pronouns

A pronoun is a word used instead of a name or noun already mentioned, or already known to the reader, in order to avoid repetition. Pronouns include 'I', 'you', 'he', 'she', 'it', 'we', 'they' and their possessive forms – I discussed the use of 'he', 'she' and 'they' on pages 109–11. (In the previous sentence, the possessive pronoun 'their' was standing in for the already-mentioned noun 'pronouns'.) The key thing about using pronouns is to make sure it is clear what noun the pronoun is standing in for. In the examples below, there is ambiguity about what the pronouns (in italics) are referring to.

> There had been a long-running rivalry between Elizabeth and Mary; now *she* started to contemplate *her* execution.

> Aristotle was a keen student of both philosophy and science. *It* was at a very preliminary stage of development.

> There are arguments both for and against the extension of democracy and representation in both Western nations and developing countries. *They* are bound to develop further.

In the final example the ambiguity is really impressive. The 'they' could refer to at least four different things, namely, 'arguments', 'democracy and representation', 'Western nations' or 'developing countries'. The ambiguity can be quite easily resolved in all three cases:

> Elizabeth had harboured a sense of rivalry with Mary for a long time; now she went further and started to contemplate her execution.

(Here the first half of the sentence makes it clear that Elizabeth is the active subject and Mary the object; this assumption is carried over into the second half of the sentence, thus clarifying the meanings of 'she' and 'her'.)

> **Aristotle was a keen student of both philosophy and science, which was at a very preliminary stage of development.**

(Here 'which was' clearly refers to the single word preceding it, namely 'science'.)

> **There are arguments both for and against the extension of democracy and representation in both Western nations and developing countries. These arguments are bound to develop further.**

(Often simply repeating the noun rather than using a pronoun is the simplest way to avoid ambiguity.)

Quotation marks

There are no fixed rules about when to use single quotation marks and when double. However, you should be consistent. If you are using double quotation marks for all quotations then a quotation within a quotation should be placed within single quotation marks; and vice versa. (See the section on 'References' on pages 119–22 for more information on quotation conventions.)

> **Goggins believes that "the most influential maxim in twentieth-century feminism is still Simone de Beauvoir's 'one is not born a woman'".**

> **Biggins writes that, 'although some theorists have preferred to talk, in the case of women, about an "Elektra complex" rather than an "Oedipus complex", this was not a usage favoured by Freud himself'.**

Sentences and non-sentences

A sentence is a set of words expressing a coherent thought and containing a subject and a verb:

> **The fox [subject] ran [verb].**

The students [subject] are shouting [verb] at their lecturer.

Immanuel Kant [subject] was [verb] the greatest German philosopher of all time.

Sometimes the subject and/or verb are simply implied. This is the case with orders and exclamations:

Go away! [Implied subject: 'you']

Horrible! [Implied subject: 'that'; implied verb: 'is']

Attention! [Implied subject: 'you'; implied verb: 'pay' or 'stand to']

The most common mistake I have come across in student essays is to present parts of sentences as if they were whole sentences, as in the following examples (where the non-sentences are in italics):

Clarence Darrow was one of the most celebrated lawyers of his generation. *Especially in the aftermath of the Scopes trial.*

(Here there is no verb in the second 'sentence'.)

The Communist party's influence gradually dwindled during the ensuing decades. *Which was seen as a victory for Capitalism.*

('Which', which refers back to a main subject, cannot itself be the subject of a sentence.)

In each of these examples the non-sentence should have been included as a qualification or sub-clause of the main sentence:

Clarence Darrow was one of the most celebrated lawyers of his generation, especially in the aftermath of the Scopes trial.

The Communist party's influence gradually dwindled during the ensuing decades, which was seen as a victory for Capitalism.

Alternatively, in each case, the non-sentence could easily be con-verted into a real sentence:

Clarence Darrow was one of the most celebrated lawyers of his generation. This was especially true in the aftermath of the Scopes trial.

> The Communist party's influence gradually dwindled during the ensuing decades. This was seen as a victory for Capitalism.

(Unlike 'which', 'this' can stand on its own as the subject of a sentence.)

Split infinitives

I was brought up by two split-infinitive purists. Each split infinitive used by a journalist or television presenter was greeted with a disapproving shake of the head. My sister and I soon learned not to split infinitives. I understand, however, that many other people have been brought up under less strict regimes *vis-à-vis* the split infinitive. Indeed, some people – although I have not yet broken this to my parents – have never even heard of the split infinitive. The world in general is somewhat more tolerant of split infinitives than it was some decades back. However, if you want to be cautious, the following are split infinitives and should be avoided: 'to boldly go'; 'to completely and utterly destroy'; 'to fully demonstrate'; 'to wholeheartedly and unreservedly subscribe'; 'to repeatedly, elaborately and intentionally split infinitives with lists of adverbs'. In all these cases the adverb should be placed either after the verb or before the 'to': 'to go boldly'; 'completely and utterly to destroy', and so on.

Tenses

Be consistent in your use of tenses. Don't switch from past to present, or vice versa, for no apparent reason, as the author does in the following example:

> The Stoic Seneca, who was a politician as well as a philosopher, says that he has no fear of death.

The policy I follow, generally, is to talk about authors of secondary texts in the present tense and authors of primary texts, and historical figures generally, in the past tense. It is very common to come across descriptions of dead writers' views in the present tense, as in: 'Kant argues that . . .', 'Machiavelli tells us that . . .'. I think it is better to put such accounts of past views in the past tense. Whatever you decide, try to be consistent.

That and which

'That' and 'which' both have many different meanings and uses. The following comments apply only to instances when they are being used to introduce clauses describing what went directly before.

'That' is used to introduce a brief and direct qualification of the word or phrase that went before. Commas are not used to separate off qualifications introduced by 'that'. You will also notice that in the first two examples below the phrases would read just as well, if not better, without 'that'. So, when reading through your work, you should be on the look-out for instances of 'that' that could be deleted.

The building that the revolutionaries stormed is still standing today.

The play that Shakespeare (allegedly) wrote was full of spelling mistakes.

Etc. is an abbreviation that is best avoided.

'Which' (or 'in which', 'to which', 'of which', and so on) is used to introduce a phrase between commas to qualify the word or phrase that went before. 'Which' introduces more incidental, elaborate or tangential qualifications than 'that'. Often 'which' means something like 'which, by the way, . . .', as in the following examples:

The central principle of Hume's epistemology, which he elaborated first of all in his *Treatise of Human Nature*, was that all knowledge is based on experience.

The chapel, in which there stands a statue of the Blessed Virgin Mary, is just over there behind those bushes.

The mind, by which Descartes meant reason and the will, was quite distinct from the body.

Their and they're

I know you all know this already (this also applies to 'who's' and 'whose', and 'your' and 'you're', below) but we all still make this slip from time to time and so it is worth reminding ourselves. 'Their' is the possessive of 'they'. 'They're' is an abbreviated form of 'they are'.

They lost their shoes while making their way through the swamp.

They're completely shoeless now that they're on the far side of the swamp.

Who's and whose

'Who's' is short for 'who is' (the apostrophe stands for the missing 'i'). 'Whose' is the possessive of 'who'.

Who's the idiot whose essay is full of basic errors?

Your and you're

'Your' is the possessive form of 'you.' 'You're' means 'you are'.

You're sick to your back teeth of being given obvious advice about grammar and spelling.

References and bibliography

The advice I have been giving so far in this chapter would apply to almost all sorts of writing, academic or otherwise. There are two important additional tools that are of particular importance to the academic – the footnote and the bibliography. These are the tools that academics use to help others track down and check the evidence supporting their argument. One of the characteristics of first-class written work is a command of referencing and bibliography.

References

Your essays should include references for all direct quotations, and for all important points and arguments that are taken directly from another source. On top of this, you should always provide a bibliography (list of books) at the end of your essay. A bibliography indicates to your reader which books you have read (and will be a helpful reminder to yourself when it comes to revision).

References can be given either in brackets in the text or in a footnote (which you can do in Microsoft® Word, by going to the 'Insert' menu, choosing 'Reference' and then choosing 'Footnote'; other packages will have a similar procedure). It is normal for the titles of books and journals to be given in italics, and for the titles of journal articles or chapters in edited books to be given inside quotation marks.

There are two main conventions for referencing. The first is to give all the relevant information (title, author, date, and page number(s) of the book or article from which the quotation or argument is taken) in the reference itself. If you are giving full references like this, it is best to put them in footnotes rather than within brackets:

> Sir James Chettam describes Casaubon as, physically, 'a shadow of a man'. 'Look at his legs!' he adds.[1] He goes on to imply a parallel between Casaubon's physical and emotional characteristics; he is a cold, dry and brittle man.[2]

> 1 George Eliot, *Middlemarch* (London: Penguin, 1985), p. 94. First published 1871–2.
> 2 *Ibid.*, pp. 94–97.

To indicate, as in the example above, that you wish to refer to the same work as in the previous footnote, use *ibid.*; to indicate that you want to refer to the same work as you cited earlier, although not in the immediately preceding references, some people use the author's surname followed by the abbreviation *op. cit.* (on these abbreviations see the section on 'Academic Latin' in Chapter 5, pages 68–72). A more pleasing alternative to *op. cit.* is to give the author's surname and an abbreviated version of the title. You could also refer the reader back to the footnote in which the full citation occurs, as in this example:

> Stefan Collini has described George Eliot's novels as providing Victorian readers with an unparalleled moral illustration of 'the self-destructive perils of selfishness'.[1] Although Eliot was not a declared follower of the positivists' 'Religion of Humanity', she certainly shared with them this advocacy of altruism within a godless yet moralistic universe.[2] The sociologist L. T. Hobouse would later recall how Eliot's novels provided a 'justification of all that it was then usual to sum up in the word altruism'.[3]

> 1 Stefan Collini, *Public Moralists: Political Thought and Intellectual Life in Britain 1850–1950* (Oxford: Clarendon Press, 1991), p. 80.
> 2 Gordon S. Haight, *George Eliot: A Biography* (Oxford: Clarendon Press, 1968), p. 390.
> 3 L. T. Hobhouse, quoted in Collini, *Public Moralists* (cited n.1), p. 89.

If you are using a quote from one author, in this case Hobhouse, that you have taken from another, in this case Collini, then you should give the reference as in the third footnote in the example. Do not reference the original text if you have not actually looked at the original.

The main alternative referencing convention is to give the surname, date and page number(s) only, in which case your reader will then refer to the bibliography at the end of the essay for fuller bibliographic information:

Stefan Collini has described George Eliot's novels as providing Victorian readers with an unparalleled moral illustration of 'the self-destructive perils of selfishness' (Collini, 1991, p. 80).

With some primary texts, which are available in many different editions, it is best to refer to the act, scene, line, chapter, section or subsection, rather than to the pages of the particular edition you are using (which you will list in the bibliography). In classic works of literature, philosophy and so on, these will be the same in all editions, in order to facilitate references even when there are many different editions in circulation. Plays and poems will have standard line numbers. Philosophical texts will often be divided into quite a lot of sections and subsections, which help with this. In the case of classic works that are available in many editions but lack this sort of standardisation (novels, for instance), there may be a standard modern edition, which your lecturer will recommend to you.

The example below makes use of a quotation from *King Lear* and gives the reference in a way that will identify the section regardless of which edition one happens to be using:

Lear and the fool subsequently have an exchange which encourages us to wonder which of them has a firmer grasp on reason:

Fool: The reason why the seven stars are no more than seven is a pretty reason.
Lear: Because they are not eight.
Fool: Yes indeed, thou would'st make a good fool.

(I.5.30–34)

It is conventional, in literary criticism, to give references to primary sources in this way (aligned with the right-hand margin, on the line below the quotation). You could also use a footnote. In this case the reference is to Act I, Scene 5, lines 30–34 of *King Lear*. The next example of citing a particular section of a classic text (rather than referring to the page numbers of a specific edition) is from an essay about the Stoics and their attitudes to emotion:

> Cicero wrote, in his *Offices*, that every action should be undertaken rationally, free from 'precipitancy on the one hand, so from all carelessness and negligence on the other'. He went on:
>
>> In order to do this, the passions must be brought under the power of reason . . . all their motions must be so quieted and restrained, as to bring no uneasiness or disturbance to the mind: and from this calm and peaceable state of the soul arises that constancy and moderation we have mentioned.
>>
>> (I.xxix)

In this case, the quotation is identified not by act, scene or line numbers but by the numbers of the sections and subsections of *The Offices* (specifically section 1, subsection 29; I followed the edition I was using in giving these numbers in roman numerals in this case).

The above example from the essay referring to Cicero also helps to illustrate a final point about how to present quotations. It is conventional to give short quotations (up to about 30 words) within quotation marks in the main body of the text, and to give longer ones separated off from the main text of the essay. Longer quotations should be in a smaller font size (10- or 11-point instead of 12-point, say) and should not be put within quotation marks. Separating them from the main text (and indenting them as in the above example) indicates that they are quotations, so they do not also need quotations marks.

When referring to a website, you need to give the name of the website, its address, and the date you accessed it:

> The French Revolution can be divided into a 'liberal' phase from 1789–91 and a 'radical' phase, from 1792 onwards, culminating in the reign of terror and the execution of Robespierre in 1794.[1]

---

1 Internet Modern History Sourcebook: <http://www.fordham.edu/halsall/mod/modsbook13.html> (accessed 19 January 2004).

Bibliography

I mentioned in Chapter 5 that it is important to keep a note of all the publication information for books and articles when you take notes from them. This is partly so that it is easy to find them again for revision or other purposes in due course. It is also to make sure that you have all the information you need to compile a bibliography. There are four main sorts of publication that you are most likely to need to include in your bibliography: books, journal articles, contributions to edited books, and websites. The bibliography should be ordered alphabetically by surname of author. Websites consulted should be listed separately at the end. The following is a short illustrative bibliography for an imagined essay about women's suffrage in Britain. The items are a journal article, a book, then a contribution to an edited book.

Bibliography

Caine, Barbara, 'Feminism, suffrage and the nineteenth-century English women's movement', *Women's Studies International Forum* 5.6 (1982), pp. 537–50.

Holton, Sandra Stanley, *Feminism and Democracy: Women's Suffrage and Reform Politics in Britain, 1900–1918* (Cambridge: Cambridge University Press, 1986).

Holton, Sandra Stanley, 'Women and the vote', in June Purvis (ed.), *Women's History: Britain 1850–1945: An Introduction* (London: Routledge, 2000), pp. 277–305.

Websites consulted

Internet women's history sourcebook: <http://www.fordham.edu/halsall/women/womensbook.html> (accessed 21 January 2004).

If you are unsure what conventions to use when referencing quotations and compiling a bibliography, look at an academic book published by a major publishing house such as Cambridge University Press, Oxford University Press, or University of Chicago Press and copy their format. Whichever convention you adopt, make sure you are consistent.

Read your work through

As well as being vigilant while writing and editing your essay, it is important also to read your essay through when you think it is finished, in order to eliminate any errors of grammar, spelling or punctuation and to make sure that all your points are clearly phrased and make sense. I know that it is very boring to read through an essay when you have just spent hours working on it and all you want to do is go to bed, go to the pub, have breakfast, or whatever. You need not read through it absolutely immediately (indeed, it is best to have a break before you do so), but you should find time at some point before you hand it in to check through it. This is important not just for assessed coursework but also for exam essays (see Chapter 11). One technique that is sadly not practicable in exams, but which can be very useful when it comes to finalising assessed coursework, is to read your work aloud, or even to get someone else to read it out to you. Having to hear your own words spoken out loud will draw your attention to incoherent sentences and tortuous phrasing extremely effectively. Whether you ask them to read it aloud or not, asking a friend to read your essay through and let you know which parts are unclear or unpersuasive is an excellent and simple way to improve your work.

Chapter 10

Writing essays and dissertations II
Arguing with style

Summary

Writing well is at the heart of academic success. Writing a good essay involves paying close attention to the title while explaining the thrust of your argument. Never start writing an essay if you cannot answer the simple question 'What is your point in this essay?'. There are several dimensions to essay-writing where you need to strike a balance: especially between other people's ideas and your own ideas, between painting the big picture and showing knowledge of details, and between giving a balanced overview and arguing for a particular point of view. Being clear, in terms both of language and of structure, is essential. Do not write in awkward over-academic prose ('essayese'); write in plain English. Your essay should include a map and signposts to direct your reader through the argument and towards the conclusion.

Now persuade your reader

By the time you sit down to write your essay, almost all the real work is done. You have worked out, from your lectures, preliminary reading or searches on the internet, what the basic scholarly dispute is, to which you are being asked to contribute. You have read the material most relevant to your topic and made notes on the views of other scholars. You have selected a few particularly nice quotations from primary (and perhaps secondary) sources. You have thought carefully and analytically about the title of your essay and have worked out an interesting argument to pursue. Finally, you have planned out the essay paragraph by paragraph. The hard work is all over!

Now you get to the fun part: working out how best to engage the attention of your reader and persuade them of your point of view; how to argue your case with style. This chapter offers advice on how to achieve this, under the following headings:

- The argument
- The evidence
- Clarity of language
- Clarity of structure.

At the very end of the chapter, I will briefly mention further additional considerations that apply when writing longer pieces of work such as dissertations.

The argument

What are the most important dos and don'ts to have in mind when choosing the words to persuade your reader? What are the most common mistakes? What are the techniques and qualities that differentiate a first-class essay from a merely competent one?

Pay close attention to the title

I have already talked about the importance of thinking carefully about your essay title, from the moment you start looking for books and articles to read onwards. Thinking about your essay title helps you decide what is the most relevant and useful reading material (see Chapter 4). It is also crucial when working out what you want to argue and planning your essay (see Chapter 7). At the stage of actually writing the essay it remains absolutely essential to pay close attention to the title. Every paragraph of your essay should be providing analysis and evidence to support your argument, which in turn should be tightly focused on the title. It should, therefore, be easy to remind the reader, from time to time, what work a particular paragraph is doing or has done to establish something relevant to the title of the essay. Think about mirroring the language of the title itself, not just in your introduction and conclusion, but during the course of the essay. In the section on 'Clarity of structure' (pages 140–1) I talk about transitional sentences at the beginning of paragraphs.

I suggest that these might be good opportunities to show you are still thinking about the question.

First-class essays are often characterised, in a way that merely competent essays are not, by a close engagement with the title and a strong sense of the relevance of each paragraph to the case being argued in response to the title. Less good essays are often character-ised by a certain looseness of relationship between title and essay. One of the most common questions I find myself asking when marking less good essays is: 'Why is he telling me this? What does it have to do with the title or his argument?' Unmotivated discussions of vaguely related material have no place in a really good essay. Stay focused on your argument and, thus, on the title.

Other people's ideas and your ideas

In putting together your case, you need to strike a balance between expositions of other people's views and your own ideas – both are very important elements of an essay. Another way of putting this is that you cannot write an essay that *both* provides an exhaustive survey of other people's ideas on a topic *and* develops your own analysis and arguments to a high level of originality and sophistication. So you need to strike a balance and make compromises. Devote a substantial amount of your essay to explaining what other people have said, but also allow a substantial amount for your own criticism and analysis of those arguments, and for developing your own arguments. It is down to you to exercise your own discretion and judgment in deciding exactly how much of each to include.

Make it clear which ideas are your own and which are borrowed from others. I sometimes read essays that initially seem to endorse two entirely opposing arguments. It often emerges that the author of the essay has failed to make it clear when they are expressing their own views and when they are explaining someone else's. A reader will assume that what they are reading is the view of the author of the essay. If it is not, then make sure it is clear whose view it is and whether or not you agree with it. If your exposition of someone else's argument goes on for several sentences, or even paragraphs, remind your reader that you are still talking about someone else's view with phrases like 'according to Hume' or 'Hume's argument continues' or 'still following Hume's line of reasoning'.

Making it clear which are you own ideas and which are someone else's is also essential if you are to avoid being guilty of plagiarism (passing off other people's writing as your own), which I will come back to in the section on 'Evidence' below.

Define your terms ... but not from a dictionary!

One way to show that you are paying close attention to the title is to pay particularly close attention to key words and phrases in the title. It will often be appropriate to offer some sort of definition of such terms. In the following essay titles I have put the key terms, which might need defining, in italics:

> Did the Italian *Renaissance* of the fifteenth century really mark a sudden break with the medieval past?
>
> Is the *problem of evil* the most substantial obstacle to belief in God?
>
> Was disagreement over the issue of slavery the principal *cause* of the American Civil War?

There is a fine line to be drawn, however, between providing useful and careful definitions of key terms on the one hand, and stating the blindingly obvious on the other. The point of defining your terms is to avoid any ambiguity or vagueness. In the case of the essay about the Renaissance, you need to be clear, for instance, about whether you are defining the Renaissance as a historical period or a cultural movement. In the essay on the problem of evil, it will be important to spell out exactly what you mean by that phrase, before assessing whether or not it threatens belief in God. And in the final example, on the American Civil War, it would be interesting to have a paragraph discussing the criteria by which historians decide upon what qualifies as a 'cause'. However, you should only offer definitions that are:

- In your own words
- A crucial underpinning for the rest of the essay
- Not vague, vacuous or obvious.

Most important of all: do not use dictionary definitions. (It is fine, of course, to look in one or more dictionaries to find out how they define the term you are interested in, but, when it comes to writing your essay, you must provide your own definition in your own words.) If a word or phrase is important enough for you to define, your reader wants to know what *you* mean by the word; not what any competent English speaker ought to mean by it according to a dictionary.

Make distinctions

One of the very best ways to show that you have understood what you have read and have thought about it clearly is to make *distinctions* between different views Showing that you are capable of making subtle distinctions between similar but importantly different arguments and points of view is a key academic skill, and one which is a characteristic of first-class work. Second-class work is more likely to fudge or overlook important differences and to rest content with rather general statements that are merely along the right lines. There are some examples of clear analytical distinctions (labelled A for analytical) below, contrasted with undifferentiated or fudged versions, given immediately after (and labelled F, for fudge). Hopefully it is clear that the version making a distinction is more interesting and sophisticated.

A: It is useful to distinguish between, on the one hand, positive sanctions, which encourage conformity by offering rewards such as increased status or community approval, and, on the other hand, negative sanctions, which punish deviance from community norms by ridicule, public shaming, or expulsion.

F: Dominant groups within a community use sanctions to encourage conformity. Sanctions are, therefore, a way for the dominant group to repress the less powerful.

A: Talking about 'the' causes of the Civil War is misleading, since the question of the cause of the war would be answered very differently in the North and in the South. It is important to distinguish between these different perspectives.

F: The main cause of the Civil War was disagreement over the issue of slavery, which divided the North against the South.

A: There was not a single 'suffragist' movement in Britain in the early twentieth century. People campaigned for 'Votes for Women' for different reasons: some as part of their campaign for greater democracy, others because they were committed to equal rights for women.

F: The beginning of the twentieth century saw an intensification of the democratic campaign for votes for women, the central focus of the women's suffragist movement.

A: The distinction that was absolutely central to Beauvoir's whole project (and indeed to much feminist thought to this day) was between sex and gender. Being a female human and being a woman are not, she said, the same thing.

F: Simone de Beauvoir argued, in *The Second Sex*, in favour of the view that you only become a woman through enculturation and social development – it is not something you are born as. Both nature and nurture, then, have to be taken into account.

The alternative, fudged versions sound like the productions of someone who is trying to disguise their ignorance. If you write essays or presentations in which you attempt to make the right sort of noises; to name the right sort of names; to use the right sort of buzz-words; but have not actually taken the material on board and analysed it for yourself, your lecturer will be able to tell. Making distinctions rather than fudging the issue with vague generalisations lets your lecturer know that you are thinking for yourself. This will encourage them to give you a first-class mark for your work if they can.

Use labels and numbers...

An excellent and simple way to bring clarity to your argument is to use labels and numbers to divide up your points. By 'labels' I mean shorthand phrases to refer to arguments or examples that you have already developed or are going to develop. In an essay on the philosophy of explanation you might want to refer to different models of explanation in shorthand terms such as 'the familiarity model' and 'the causal model'. In an essay about the nineteenth-century women's movement, you might want to give labels to different groups: 'the feminists', 'the suffragists' and 'the radicals'. In an essay on theories of emotions, you could talk about three main classes of theory: 'judgement theories', 'feeling theories' and 'component theories'.

A technique I particularly favour as a way to help myself and my readers through what I have written is to use numbers. If you say at the start of your essay that you will be looking at three different groups within the nineteenth-century women's movement, or three different theories of emotion, then your reader will be able to keep track of them as they go through the essay, and will have a sense of how far they have got and how much further they have to go. Using numbers, like using labels, also indicates a command of the material. Knowing that you specifically have two, three or four objections to a particular argument indicates that you have thought about this in precise terms and know exactly what you need to tell the reader.

... but not big numbers

Using numbers *can* indicate mastery of your material. However, if the numbers involved are too large they can tend instead to indicate that you have been quite swamped by your material and have failed to analyse and prioritise your points adequately. Far from giving a sense of confidence and control, the following could give a sense of a somewhat chaotic essay in the offing:

> There are nine reasons why this preliminary definition is not acceptable.

> In this essay I have sixteen main points.

Specific points not sweeping generalisations

Sweeping generalisations (other than this one) are bad things. Always be as specific and precise as possible. If you think that you can make your point more specific, then do so. The following are examples of the sort of thing to be avoided.

> In the seventeenth century, philosophers agreed that the universe was a clockwork machine.

> The Catholic church has always been more hostile to science than the Protestant churches.

> Postmodern critics agree that there is no essential subjective 'self'.

Instead of relying on sweeping generalisations (even ones that you might have heard your lecturer use in lectures or seminars), try to refer to specific individuals, specific events and specific arguments. Show your awareness of the subtle differences between the various approaches that have been taken to different questions in the past and the present. Which seventeenth-century philosophers did you have in mind? Which events show evidence of a Catholic hostility to science? Which literary critics fall under your category of 'post-modern'? Which of them agree with the statement in question and which do not?

Analysis and synthesis

Academic writers have two principal tasks: analysis and synthesis. Analysis is the job of breaking down big questions and facts into smaller ones and providing specific, detailed and exact descriptions and arguments. The end result of analysis is often to make the object of study seem very complicated, multi-faceted, messy and diffuse. Synthesis is the job of rebuilding the many contingent, diffuse facts into clear statements of general principles, guiding narratives and universal trends. Undergraduate essays generally contain too much synthesis and not enough analysis.

Synthesis is a luxury to which you must earn the right. You have to show that you know about the messy contingent details in question before you can justifiably make synthetic declarations about general trends in the history of thought or make grand statements about literature, society, science, philosophy, religion and culture. The way that you earn that right is by doing *analysis*; that is to say, by learning specific, detailed facts and arguments. Synthetic statements not backed up by an analysis of the relevant facts and arguments are empty.

You need to strike a balance between showing your awareness of the big picture and showing that you are capable of fine-grained analysis. The introductory and concluding sections of your essay are normally the best places to show your awareness of the big picture – of the main issues and the main protagonists in the discussions or period you are writing about. In the rest of the essay, rather than trying to be exhaustive (which would be absolutely impossible even if it were desirable, which it is not), you should pick a few key points, whether they be particular historical events, or particular arguments, or particular individual thinkers, or particularly suggestive or problematic words in the essay title, and engage in a much closer analysis of them. So, in the body of your essay, you should be showing that you can think rigorously and analytically about quite specific ideas, rather than painting a big exhaustive picture of the topic in vague and general terms. Being aware of this need to keep the right balance between the big picture and detailed, close analysis is essential to writing good essays and to avoiding writing in a vague and sweeping way, which is a tendency found all too often in second- and third-class essays.

The evidence

The two most important questions that you must be able to answer in relation to an academic essay, dissertation or presentation are:

- What is your argument? (See the previous section.)
- What is your evidence?

Two of the best ways to provide evidence for and illustrations of your arguments are quotations and examples. I have never read an essay that had too many interesting quotations or too many good examples. I have often read essays that contained none of either. However, you should avoid going to the other extreme of simply stringing quotations or examples together in an unanalysed list.

Quotations

As I said in Chapter 5, you should choose quotations from primary or secondary sources that are either particularly well-expressed ideas or good examples of a view that you wish to endorse or dispute. Make it clear what they illustrate and what you think of them. As I also said in Chapter 5, it is much more likely that you will want to include quotations from primary texts than from secondary discussions. More often than not, it will be better to use paraphrases from secondary sources. The main thing you should *not* use quotations from secondary sources for is simply to state a basic point you want to make yourself. The following examples illustrate this. In each case the quotation does not add any particular clarity or authority to the point being made. Rather, it is there as a lazy alternative to putting the point in one's own words (which would, in these cases, have been a preferable alternative), or even to thinking of one's own point at all. It is an unprocessed lump of someone else's writing, borrowed without analysis:

> As Giddens has pointed out, 'The study of deviance, like other fields of sociology, directs our attention to social *power*, as well as the influence of social class – the divisions between rich and poor. . . . As

> we shall see, social norms are strongly influenced by divisions of
> power and class.'[1]

> As Barbara Caine says, 'The essential individualism of mid-century
> liberalism, with its notion of men as rational and self-interested
> beings and its belief in the importance of men following their own
> perceived self-interests, provided the foundation for the demands of
> the movement'.[2]

So, what are appropriate ways to use quotations from secondary
sources? The first thing to say is that they should be brief. They can
sometimes be used, if they include a particularly striking or pleasing
turn of phrase, to add colour and a different voice from your own to
your essay, perhaps in the introduction or conclusion, as in the
following opening paragraph of an essay:

> Peter J. Parish uses a theatrical metaphor to describe the American
> 'Civil War tragedy'. If economic and social change were the back-
> drop, he says, and disagreements over the constitution were the
> stage directions, then 'the plot was provided by Negro slavery'.[3] In
> this essay I will suggest, to extend but challenge Parish's metaphor,
> that Negro slavery in fact provided little more than the costumes in
> a drama where the main protagonists were economic and political.

Another useful thing that quotations can be used for is to provide
definitions – not so much as a way to pin down a single definitive
meaning of a difficult concept, but as a way to pin down a particular
author. If a significant part of your essay will involve agreeing with or
criticising an important author, it is essential that you represent their
views precisely and fairly. The following is an example of a quotation
of this sort:

> Giddens' definition of deviance is 'non-conformity to a given set of
> norms that are accepted by a significant number of people in a

---

1 Anthony Giddens, *Sociology*, 3rd edn (Oxford: Polity/Blackwell, 1997), p. 173.
2 Barbara Caine, 'Feminism, suffrage and the nineteenth-century English women's
   movement', *Women's Studies International Forum* 5.6 (1982), pp. 537–50; quotation
   from p. 540.
3 Peter J. Parish, *The American Civil War* (London: Eyre Methuen, 1975), p. 88.

community or society'.[4] This sounds reasonable but, as we shall see below, it is very difficult to be precise about what exactly constitutes a 'significant number of people' in a given community. It is also difficult to specify what are legitimate ways for the 'significant number of people' to impose their norms on those who disagree with them.

Plagiarism

Your department and university will have a plagiarism policy with which you must familiarise yourself. It is very straightforward. If there is any suggestion that you are trying to pass off someone else's work (such as an essay you downloaded from the internet, borrowed from another student, or lifted from an academic book or journal) as your own, you could get into very serious trouble; you could even be kicked out of your university. I mention this here, since one of the ways you could end up being accused of plagiarism is if you failed to use quotation marks around material taken from secondary sources, and failed to give references to those sources. Some students fail to do these things, not in an attempt to pass off others' work as their own, but out of carelessness. However, this sort of carelessness in an important piece of assessed work could land you in a lot of trouble. So – be sure to use quotation marks and give references on the relatively rare occasions when you want to quote directly from secondary sources.

Clarity of language

Plain English not 'essayese'

Lots of people, when they come to write an essay, start thinking and writing in 'essayese' rather than in English. Essayese is a mysterious, over-formal, unnatural, and cumbersome foreign language. It is not actually taught in any school or university that I know of, but it is tacitly learned in an as yet unexplained way during people's teenage years. I fear that schoolteachers may have something to do with it. Some of the blame, however, must also lie with university academics, who, during the course of the twentieth century, conspired to

4 Giddens, *Sociology*, p. 173.

develop an increasingly unreadable prose style. More and more, the lively yet precise prose of great eighteenth- and nineteenth-century essayists, historians and philosophers was supplanted by a jargonistic, pedestrian and impenetrable sort of specialist academic discourse. I think this 'acadmic expertese' may be the ultimate source of the essayese which I often find myself complaining about in student essays today. (I should, to be fair to my profession, to avoid being branded a traitor, and for the sake of accuracy, add that most academics these days write extremely well; it is only a minority who produce obscure, jargonistic, pompous, excessively abstract, or pretentious prose of the sort that gives us all a bad name.)

Essayese reads rather like a bad translation of a foreign language into English by someone with a grasp of neither the foreign language nor English. In essayese, the English phrase 'I think' is replaced by odd phrases such as 'it is arguable to propound the view that', or 'it can be reasonably propagated that', or 'the argument that is being postulated here is that'. Essayese phrases for the English phrase 'This argument is wrong' include 'This point of view must be seen by us here as being utterly fallacious' and 'We must observe that this flawed position is nonsensical and can obviously not be allowed to be upheld'. Essayese terms for the perfectly good English words 'says', 'states', or 'argues' include 'expounds', 'propounds', 'opines', 'decrees', 'affirms', 'proclaims', 'dictates', 'insists', 'assures us', 'reminds us'. Of course, it is good to expand your vocabulary, which is why your schoolteachers may have encouraged you to use synonyms such as these; however, from a stylistic point of view, relentless use of synonyms of this kind sounds forced and unnatural.

Don't worry about using words like 'wrong' and 'false' or like 'says' and 'argues' too often. They are words that will often need to be used in an academic essay. It is much better to use these same plain English words several times than to use forced and unnatural alternatives just for the sake of variety. I have never decreed, propagated, propounded, or expounded anything in my life; but I have thought, said, and argued many things.

One way that you might end up using essayese phrases and sentences is if you try to adopt an 'academic' style of writing rather than your own normal way of thinking and talking. When you are set an academic essay, you are *not* being asked to switch into a special 'academic' way of thinking and writing. You are, rather, being asked to think, assess evidence, and write in a natural and straightforward way. You are not required to adopt a pompous jargon-ridden style.

Nor are you being asked to write long convoluted sentences. Write sentences *in your own words*. And never write something that you do not understand simply because you think it sounds like the sort of thing you are supposed to say.

Another very good way to avoid writing in essayese is to aspire to avoid the passive voice. Here are some examples of passive phrases:

It can be persuasively argued that . . .

From one point of view it could be stated that . . .

It should be emphasised that . . .

These are suitable active alternatives:

I argue that . . .

In my view . . .

Remember that . . .

Hopefully you can immediately see how much clearer and sharper the prose is in the active phrases. It is often just as good to do away with passive phrases altogether. Rather than replacing them with active phrases, you will often find that the prose reads better if they are just cut out. Here are some sentences using passive phrases:

It can be persuasively argued that Marx was the most influential thinker of the nineteenth century.

From one point of view it could be stated that economics is not a science at all.

It should be emphasised that London was, at this stage, the largest city in the world.

And here they are again with the passive phrases removed:

Marx was the most influential thinker of the nineteenth century.

Some say that economics is not a science at all.

London was, at this stage, the largest city in the world.

Essayese, in addition to making excessive use of the passive voice, contains lots of superfluous adverbs. As a general rule, be sparing in your use of the following:

- 'Probably', 'basically' (these add nothing, make you look unsure of what you are saying, and sound rather colloquial).
- 'Clearly', 'obviously', 'inevitably' (the arguments and claims that you will be evaluating in your essay are very unlikely to be 'clearly', 'obviously', or 'inevitably' true or false, convincing or unconvincing – these adverbs are too often used in the place of a good explanation of why a position is right or wrong).
- 'Incredibly', 'amazingly', 'unbelievably' (as well as sounding sloppy and colloquial, these are almost always excessive – a simple 'very' or, sometimes, 'extremely' will normally do the trick – don't gush!).

Of course it is true that writing an essay requires a more structured and formal use of language than would be appropriate for, for instance, having a chat with a friend in the pub. However, as a general guideline, the following is useful: never use in an essay a word or phrase that you would not dream of using in conversation with a friend.

Indeed, one of the best tips is to imagine, when writing your essay, that you are explaining the topic and your argument to a friend who knows very little about the subject. If you have actually talked to a friend about the essay before you write it (see Chapter 7) then this should be all the more straightforward to accomplish.

Choose your words carefully

Too many people, at least implicitly, believe that words are disposable and interchangeable vehicles for ideas. This is a mistaken view of the relationship between words and ideas. Your words are not the vehicles for your ideas – they *are* your ideas. If you can't say it clearly, you don't understand it. In other words, a confusingly worded argument is not the result of someone with a clear understanding of an argument choosing the wrong words. Rather, it is the result of someone lacking a clear understanding of the argument. Confused ideas and confused words are the same things; using language well and thinking well are the same thing.

Being *clear* and being *simplistic* are not the same thing. The best arguments, when put forward by the best writers, are often both subtle and clear; both intellectually challenging and lucid. Do not think that a clear and transparent argument is a simplistic argument; it is a well-expressed argument. Aspire to clarity, not to obscurity. As the Victorian essayist and Darwinian, Thomas Huxley, put it: 'Obscurity is more often the result of the muddiness rather than of the depth of the stream of thought'.[5]

Since essays are about showing that you have understood ideas, it is essential that the words/ideas you choose are the right ones. After each word, each sentence, each paragraph you should ask yourself, 'Is that *exactly* what I meant? Do those words together form a clear and coherent idea? Or has my choice of words produced an ambiguous, wordy, obscure or clumsy sentence?'

Never write something in an essay that you don't understand yourself!

Often you might end up writing something you don't understand if it is a phrase or sentence you have heard in a lecture, or read in a book, and which you think sounds good, despite not having much idea what it means. Do not reproduce the phrases and constructions used by the authors you are discussing when giving an account of their views (other than when you are quoting from them, of course). Mixing their phrases with your own almost always results in awkward and unnatural writing. Use your own words. Putting ideas into your own words ensures not only that you write more clearly but also that you have understood the point. More often than not, the reason why we resort to using someone else's words is that we don't quite know how to put the point ourselves, because we don't really understand it. This is another example of how clear writing and clear thinking are two sides of the same coin.

Finally, be prepared to rewrite sentences. Writing on a word-processor makes it easier to do this. Your first attempt at a sentence will often be awkward or unclear and in need of revision or rephrasing.

Such perfectionism about choice of words can be time-consuming initially, but it is the essential basis of an excellent writing (and hence thinking) technique. With time, good choice of words becomes

---

5 Thomas Huxley's review in 1854 of the anonymous *Vestiges of the Natural History of Creation*, available online at the 'Huxley File': <http://aleph0.clarku.edu/huxley/SM5/vest.html> (accessed 20 April 2004).

second nature. This is all excellent training for your exams, when you will need to choose the right words quickly and under pressure.

Clarity of structure

There is resistance among some students, and some academics, to transparent and straightforward structure and signposting in essays. A lot of people think that an essay including sentences such as, for instance, 'In this essay I will be making three points' is a *childish* or *unstylish* essay. I disagree. I think an essay that indicates at the outset what points will be made, makes them, summarises the case and provides a conclusion – with each new stage in the essay signposted – is a *clear* essay. I have never read an essay and thought to myself 'This is dreadful – it's just too clear' or 'This is a good essay, but I just wish the arguments weren't so lucidly signposted'. A clear essay is a good essay; and explicit structure and signposting, I believe, are among the most effective ways to make your essay clear and your arguments transparent.

If you think of your essay as being a stretch of terrain, one of your duties as a writer is to provide your readers with a map of the terrain, and signposts to facilitate their journey through it. Your introduction should include a basic map. It is also a good idea to include several transitional sentences in the course of your essay that act as signposts, telling readers where they have got to and how far they still have to go, as in the examples below. Rhetorical questions can make particularly effective transitional sentences. These are also useful opportunities to show that you are still focusing on the title of the essay:

A second problem with conflict theories of crime is that they do not allow for the fact that each individual is a member of many different social groups.

The third and final reason to think that slavery was a pretext for war rather than a cause of war is that slavery was a moribund social institution at the time.

But what about the more everyday, domestic concerns of Victorian women – how did they relate to the campaign for women's suffrage?

What, then, is the textual evidence supporting this supposedly close connection between the polarities of blindness/vision and madness/sanity in *King Lear*?

Without a map and signposts, like these transitional senten
lers through your essay are likely to get lost and disorien

Paragraphs

The paragraph is the basic building block of every essay. Think
about what constitutes a paragraph rather than simply starting a new
one when you have written about fifteen or twenty lines and feel
like the paragraph is looking rather too long. Each paragraph should
make just one point, or sub-point, or at least have a single clear
theme, which is illustrated with a couple of examples and/or quotations. As a general rule, paragraphs should not be much longer than
about half of a page. They can be much shorter if the point is a short
and snappy one. It is often a good idea to start a paragraph with a
transitional sentence or with a sentence stating the topic of that
paragraph. For example, this paragraph started with a very simple
'topic sentence' indicating the theme of the whole paragraph: 'The
paragraph is the basic building block of every essay.' Below are
examples of paragraphs, with the topic sentence in italics. Note that
in both these cases, the topic sentence comes at the end instead of
the beginning of the paragraph, as a summary or culmination of
what the paragraph has been building towards:

> We all know who deviants are, or so we tend to think. Devi-
> ants are those individuals who refuse to live by the rules that
> the majority of us follow. They're violent criminals, drug
> addicts, or 'down-and-outs', who don't fit in with what most
> people would define as normal standards of acceptability. Yet
> things are not quite as they appear − a lesson sociology often
> teaches us, for it encourages us to look beyond the obvious.
> *The notion of the deviant, as we shall see, is actually not an easy one
> to define.*[6]

> Semmelweis's research is a simple and striking illustration of
> inferences to the best explanation in action, and of the way
> they exploit contrastive data. It is also Hempel's paradigm of
> the hypothetico-deductive method. So this case is particularly
> well suited for a comparison of the virtues of Inference to the

6 Giddens, *Sociology*, p. 172.

Best Explanation and the deductive model. *The example, I suggest, shows that Inference to the Best Explanation is better than hypothetico-deductivism.*[7]

Beginnings

The two most important paragraphs of any essay, dissertation or article are the first and the last. Let's begin at the beginning. People disagree about how to start an essay. Starting with the basics, I think there are two things an introductory section should do. Each is a sort of mapping exercise, the first on a larger scale than the second:

- *The big picture.* Give an overview of the topic and a flavour of why it is an interesting or controversial one; sketch the big picture. Indicate where the particular piece of terrain you cover in your essay is located in the wider area.
- *The map.* Provide a more detailed map of your particular piece of terrain. State what you are going to say in your essay. Specifically, state what form the essay will take – what your main points are and the order in which you are going to cover them – and also (possibly) state briefly the conclusion you are working towards. Sometimes it might be effective to wait until the end to unveil an unexpected conclusion. Generally, though, the mystery story is not a particularly good model for the academic essay.

Below is an example of an introduction to an essay achieving both these basic things.

What features of Darwin's theory of evolution were the most difficult to reconcile with Christian belief?

It is often said that the Victorian age was one in which Christian belief was in 'crisis'. Traditional religious beliefs were assailed from many quarters, including radical politics, Comtean philosophy, and biblical criticism. It is, however, science in general and Darwin's theory of evolution in particular that are remembered as representing the biggest challenges to Christian faith and engendering the most

7 Peter Lipton, *Inference to the Best Explanation* (London and New York: Routledge, 1991), p. 88.

passionate debates on the subject during the nineteenth century. The question that this essay will address is why exactly Darwin's theory was thought to be in conflict with the Christian religion.

I will consider three ways in which Darwin's theory of evolution was difficult to reconcile with Christianity. I will start by looking at how it contradicted a literal reading of the Bible. Secondly, I will explain how Darwin's theory undermined Enlightenment natural theology. Thirdly, I will discuss the conflict between Darwin's 'continuist' view of nature and the traditional Christian belief that there is a qualitative distinction between human beings and the 'brute creation'. Finally, I will conclude that, especially in terms of how it changed accepted views about the origins and status of human beings (and of human morality), Darwin's theory was difficult to reconcile with Christianity principally because it was part of what was, in fact, a competing 'religion', namely the broader agnostic-materialist worldview of Victorian science.

I think some people are resistant to the idea of providing this sort of introduction as they think it makes their essay sound somehow juvenile or unsophisticated. However, professional academics very often use exactly this style of introduction in their conference papers, journal articles and books. It is simply a great help to the audience or reader to tell them where you are going. Consider the following introductory 'map' sentences from two academic articles, on the themes of the Victorian women's movement and madness in Shakespeare's plays, respectively:

In this article I propose to look at the ideology, the strategy and the style of the women's movement in order to explore the relationship between them, and the discrepancies which sometimes existed between the ultimate aims of the movement and the measures it adopted.[8]

I want to argue in this essay that Shakespeare's presentation of madness in *Hamlet* and more particularly in *King Lear* is more

8 Barbara Caine, 'Feminism, suffrage and the nineteenth-century English women's movement', *Women's Studies International Forum* 5.6 (1982), pp. 537–50; quotation from p. 538.

searching and realistic than that of many of his fellow playwrights, that the reasons for this are more specific than simply
his superior genius, and that recent work in social history can
give us an insight into what makes Shakespeare's vision special.[9]

While it is certainly neither unstylish nor simplistic to tell your
reader where your essay or article is going, it might be best for this
not to be the *very first* thing you do. I have noticed that these sorts
of 'map' sentences tend to creep in after a paragraph or two in
professional academics' articles. So, what other, more sophisticated
techniques are available to use at the very start of an essay?

I think there are two main ways that many academics try to
combine stylishness with helpfulness in the opening section of an
article. In each case their 'map' (of the 'In this article I will show . . .'
variety) is preceded by something else, namely a 'big picture', and/or
one or both of the following:

• A 'set piece'. This might be an account of a telling historical
  episode. Or it could be a particularly nice quotation from a
  primary source. The idea of a set piece is to set the tone for the
  whole article; to introduce the reader to the main theme in an
  arresting or entertaining way; or to transport the reader to a
  particular time and place. A favourite trick of historians is to use
  a very specific event to introduce a general theme. The following is the opening paragraph of an essay on slavery and the
  American Civil War. Notice how the opening paragraph has the
  effect of transporting the reader right to the heart of the political
  struggles of the time, mainly thanks to the use of the original
  words of one of the key protagonists:

  > During the first month of the Civil War, Jefferson Davis
  > presented to the Confederate Congress a straightforward
  > justification for secession and a now-classic explanation of
  > the war's origins. Over the decades, Davis explained, the
  > South's slave labour force has 'convert[ed] hundreds of
  > thousands of square miles of wilderness into cultivated lands

---

9 Alexander Leggatt, 'Madness in *Hamlet, King Lear*, and early modern England', in
Jay L. Halio (ed.), *Critical Essays on Shakespeare's* King Lear (New York: G. K. Hall
& Co., 1996), pp. 122–38; quotation from p. 122.

covered with a prosperous people,' while 'the productions in the South of cotton, rice, sugar, and tobacco . . . had swollen to an amount which formed nearly three-quarters of the exports of the whole United States and had become absolutely necessary to the wants of civilized man.' 'For the full development and continuance' of such achievements, Davis stressed, 'the labor of African slaves was and is indispensable.' Naturally, then, 'with interests of such over-whelming magnitude imperilled,' secession was necessary.[10]

- A 'burning platform'. This is a more sophisticated, scholarly version of the 'big picture'; it identifies a particular problem of interpretation or a scholarly dispute. The basic structure of a burning platform is often: 'Scholars until recently always said X. But now a group of revisionists say Y. Which position is correct?' The second paragraph of the chapter about slavery and the American Civil War, the opening paragraph of which I just quoted, is a burning platform. It starts with the sentence: 'After decades of scholarly struggle, the prevailing interpretation of the war's causes follows Davis's speech in placing slavery at centre stage.' The rest of the paragraph discusses reasons to be sceptical about this interpretation and indicates that the rest of the chapter will reflect and adjudicate upon these different scholarly points of view.[11]

Experiment for yourself with different ways to start an essay. Speaking from the point of view of someone who regularly marks assessed essays, dissertations and exam essays, I cannot tell you how welcome it is to pick up a script and find that its author has made an effort to engage your attention, arouse your interest, provide you with a thought-provoking, arresting or unexpected opening paragraph or two. If this attention-grabbing opening is followed by or includes an account of a key scholarly dispute to which the essay relates, and a brief map of the essay itself, then, speaking for myself,

---

10 Bruce Levine, ' "What did we go to war for?" Confederate emancipation and its meaning', in Susan-Mary Grant and Brian Holden Reid (eds), *The American Civil War: Explorations and Reconsiderations* (Harlow: Longman, 2000), pp. 239–64; quotation from p. 239.
11 Levine, 'What did we go to war for?', pp. 239–40.

I will be so overwhelmingly grateful that I will be predisposed to give the essay a first if I possibly can.

Just to recap: the key components of the introductory section to an essay (of which you should normally include two or more) are:

- ˙ Set piece
- Burning platform and/or big picture
- Map.

Finally, in case you are thinking that in a short essay, or an essay written in examination conditions, you do not have the time or space for such an elaborate opening section, let me reassure you that you can include two or more of the above components in a single short paragraph, as in the following example, which is the first paragraph of an article about George Eliot's *Middlemarch*:

> Everybody says that *Middlemarch* is a great work. Many of its original reviewers said that it raised the Woman Question. Yet the body of criticism from then till now makes surprisingly little case for it as a great feminist work. I think it is.[12]

In four elegant sentences the author has provided: the big picture, in the first sentence; a burning platform (the scholarly puzzle of why little has been said about *Middlemarch* and feminism), in the second and third sentences; and, finally, if not exactly a map, then at least a wonderfully concise indication of the direction of her argument, in that final four-word sentence. What a good introduction!

The simplest way of all to provide an arresting and interesting opening to an essay, which also implicitly indicates the direction the whole essay will take, is to have a one-sentence first paragraph that answers the question in an unexpected way. This will alert your reader at once to the fact that they have in front of them an unusually interesting essay; as in the following examples:

Were the Stoics against the emotions?

The Stoics were not against the emotions, because the 'emotions' was not a category any Stoic philosopher ever used; instead they

---

12 Kathleen Blake, '*Middlemarch* and the Woman Question', *Nineteenth-Century Fiction* 31.3 (1976), pp. 285–312; quotation from p. 285.

distinguished between troubling passions and more calm positive feelings, which they termed *eupatheia*.

Is the problem of evil the most substantial obstacle to belief in God?

The so-called 'problem of evil' is not a problem at all; in fact the concept of God – the supreme Good – can only make sense in a world which is both good and evil.

Endings

So much for beginnings, what about endings? I have discovered that there is a widely felt desire amongst undergraduate students to make a personal policy statement in the final paragraph of an essay, regardless of the essay title; people like to end an essay with a sweeping personal manifesto about the way to solve all the problems of literature, science, philosophy, ethics, politics, or theology. This is not a good idea.

There is one particularly popular personal manifesto: relativism. The relativist asserts that everyone's beliefs are equally valid. On this view, we all 'feel' different things about intellectual issues; and no amount of evidence can really change the way we feel. There are some examples of relativist conclusions below.

Some people think that science supports religious belief but science can be taken in an infinite number of different ways depending on what one feels. It all just depends on your prior beliefs, and each interpretation is equally valid.

To conclude, we cannot make dogmatic distinctions between the opinions of Marxists and other sociologists; it depends on how you interpret them whether you feel they are in opposition to each other or not.

Some have interpreted *King Lear* as an anti-feminist play. There is much evidence to back this up. But it all depends on one's personal attitude to feminist theory. I feel that the controversy has been exaggerated out of proportion really.

You could, indeed, conclude that Eliot's *Middlemarch* was a manifesto for altruism. But some argued that complete altruism was not

> a good thing or not even possible. It depends whether you feel complete altruism is possible or not, which is, I feel, a matter of opinion (although I personally think that altruism must be the foundation of a just society). In our selfish and competitive secular world, it is certainly hard to find evidence of true altruism today, which is a sign of the postmodern predicament.

The final paragraph of your essay should not contain a sweeping personal manifesto, relativist or otherwise; rather it should contain a summary of the way that you have approached the question and a clear statement of your answer to the question. *Always answer the question.* If you do not answer the question you will be heavily penalised, whether in an exam or in a piece of coursework. Your conclusion should do two main things: first, it should recapitulate and summarise what you have said – naming the most important arguments and examples; secondly, it should provide a clear synthetic statement of your position – the position for which the arguments and examples you have just summarised are providing support – which should be a direct response to the essay title. It is sometimes a good idea to repeat the question at the start of your last paragraph.

The other reason why the 'relativist' manifesto is an unsatisfactory position to take when writing an academic essay is that it is a way of avoiding actually producing and evaluating the *arguments* for and against a particular position. It is not good enough to say that it just depends what you think or that ultimately we cannot have a certain answer. In an academic essay you are required to analyse the arguments and the evidence put forward by various different people and explain why you think that one position is more or less reasonable and persuasive than another position. *It is not true that all positions are equally valid.* Some are more reasonable than others; some are better supported by textual evidence, historical facts or sociological data than others.

Sentences

The paragraph is the building block of every essay; the sentence is the building block of every paragraph. Academics disagree amongst themselves about sentences. Some favour short ones. Others are quite happy, indeed enthusiastic, about the idea that students should, in the course of their studies, cultivate the art of the long sentence; being able to retain control of one's ideas and language while constructing a complex and involved sentence, making judicious use of commas and semicolons, they say, is an important academic skill. I prefer brevity. There is no need to adopt a hard and fast rule about this, though. Sometimes a long and involved sentence might be appropriate and attractive. In my experience of reading and marking student essays, however, their sentences seem to be too long more often than they are too short. So, I only want to concentrate on the virtues of the (relatively) short sentence. I hope that the examples below illustrate the improved clarity that can be achieved by breaking a long sentence down into two or more shorter ones. Here is a long sentence:

> In this essay I will focus on the ideas of the socialist movement on reproduction, as an issue which was not only of great interest to the socialist movement, but shows the extent to which it incorporated late-Victorian scientific ideology into its own outlook.

It is straightforward to break this up into three shorter sentences:

> In this essay I will focus on the ideas of the socialist movement on reproduction. Reproduction was an issue of great concern to them. This concern shows how the movement incorporated late-Victorian scientific ideology into its own outlook.

The following sentence is *really* long:

> This essay is an exploration of those two features of *King Lear* which have, perhaps, most often been thought of as its defining themes – both at the time and in more recent criticism – namely two very human physico-moral failings signified in the play in connected ways, which are the literal human inability to see physical reality in all its varieties of light and shade, colour and pattern (blindness), and also the moral and intellectual inability to perceive human social relations for what they really are, in all their different tones and hues, particularly urgent in this period of political crisis (madness).

Once again we can break it up, this time into four shorter sentences:

> This essay is an exploration of two features of *King Lear* which have often been thought of as its defining themes, both at the time and in

more recent criticism. The first is the literal human inability to see physical reality in all its varieties of light and shade, colour and pattern (blindness). The second is also a sort of blindness: the moral and intellectual inability to perceive human social relations for what they really are, in all their different tones and hues (madness). The failure of social vision was a particularly urgent problem in this period of political crisis.

Extended essays and dissertations

The above advice on structure, language and argumentation all also applies when it comes to producing assessed essays and dissertations. There are also a few specific additional points to bear in mind. Longer pieces of written work (from 5,000 up to 15,000 words) require more careful planning and structuring. Think about using subsections and subheadings to help make it clear what is going on, and what work each section is doing. Never forget to keep asking yourself: 'What is my point, and how does the material in this section or subsection support or illustrate my point?' As with all your work, it is essential that you have a clear and original line of argument, rather than just a collection of quotations – even if there are dozens of them and they are all fascinating. By the time you are planning and writing the first draft of a dissertation you must be able to give a lucid and succinct answer to the question 'What's your point?'. Your answer will refer both to an ongoing scholarly dispute and the evidence you think is most important in resolving it.

When writing extended assessed work you may have several meetings with the same lecturer or tutor over a period of several weeks. Make sure that you make the best use of these meetings. You and your lecturer should both be clear at the outset what your project is (this should be decided by the two of you in consultation), how many times you are going to meet, at what intervals, when you will be submitting to your lecturer a first draft of the essay or dissertation, and when it needs to be finished by. If your lecturer does not raise these issues with you, you should raise them yourself.

You will be expected to show considerably broader and deeper understanding of a subject in an assessed extended essay or a dissertation than would be the case in an assessed essay of 2,000 or 3,000 words. It is supremely important when producing extended and assessed written work to read primary texts rather than relying on secondary discussions, and to read around the field rather than relying on the first source you come across. Work out how the material you are writing about has been interpreted in different ways by authoritative and influential scholars in the field. Your lecturer will be able to help direct you towards the right editions of the most important primary texts and the most relevant and interesting secondary works. This broader reading process will provide you with an opportunity to make use of the wide range of books, manuscripts, journals, PhD theses, and electronic databases available in your departmental and university libraries.

In the case of extended essays and dissertations it is normally a requirement that they should be word-processed. It is also worth thinking about presentation more generally. Examiners like to read essays and dissertations that are aesthetically pleasing as well as academically excellent. Think about how to set out the text in terms of margins, spacing and so on, perhaps include a separate title page, and some illustrations.

Finally, it is absolutely essential in an extended essay or dissertation to provide proper 'scholarly apparatus'; this means giving references to primary and secondary sources (in footnotes) and a full bibliography of the works you consulted, giving author, date, title, place of publication and publisher. Follow the conventions of an established academic publisher (and see the section at the end of Chapter 9 on references and bibliographies).

Chapter 11

Revision and exams

Summary

Everyone has their own favoured way of revising. But there are several techniques that most people will find effective, such as making a revision timetable, looking at past papers, and writing practice answers. It is also a good idea to read new material. Think about what you can commit to memory before going into an exam. In the exam, make sure you have read the instructions properly and that you have looked at both sides of every sheet of the question paper. Be clear in your mind how much time you have for each question, and stick to it. The two most important things: answer the question and don't be boring!

Should you be stressed?

What most people think of when they think of exams, especially important ones, is stress, anxiety and fear. As with giving a presentation, there is a certain amount of fear and apprehension about exams that is both perfectly natural and potentially advantageous if it motivates you to make sure you are well prepared. And, as with presentations and all the other tasks we have been discussing so far, the key to success is proper preparation. In this case, by 'proper preparation', I do not mean the last few weeks of revision before the exams, but the semester, year or years leading up to the exam period. If, over that period, you have worked out what the key questions are in each course you are taking; have looked at old exam papers and paid attention to the course documentation; have attended and paid attention to your lectures and seminars; have made useful and well-organised notes; and have read around the subject and thought carefully about what your line is on the central issues; then you do not have too much to worry about. Hopefully this will be the case, and so you will be able to approach the final period of revision in a relatively calm state of mind. If you have not done these things, then you will have more reason to feel scared.

If you are particularly averse to exams as a form of assessment, you can try to choose courses that are assessed mainly, or entirely, by coursework rather than exams (see Chapter 2).

Vision and revision

So, as you enter this relatively calm period of final revision for a course, what are the best ways to use your time? One of the most effective forms of revision is to read *new* material that you have not looked at before (this is not, strictly speaking, *re*vision at all – you could just call it 'vision').

The best things to look at are books and articles that you couldn't get hold of when you worked on the topic the first time round; or that you didn't have time to read as closely or deeply as you would have liked; or books that are a little more advanced; or even books that are slightly tangential to the topic.

The way to choose what books to read is to look back at reading lists, or to ask your lecturer, or simply to browse in the library looking for anything that grabs your interest. Many libraries have displays of their new acquisitions – these are often particularly interesting. The reasons why it is important to read new material when revising are as follows:

- Your thinking will be re-stimulated – new books will pose new questions and new challenges to reawaken your thoughts on a given topic. When it comes to the exam your essays will have a greater chance of being fresh and alive, rather than just being reheated versions of ideas you had months or years ago.
- The notes and essay that you wrote the first time round were produced many months previously, when your whole outlook and understanding were less well developed. They are thus stuck at a relatively basic level, and revising them will only reacquaint you with these relatively underdeveloped ideas and ways of

thinking. Reading new material provides you with an opportunity to frame the topic in a more advanced and subtle way.
* Revising old notes and essays is relatively dull. Reading new material is more fun and will make revision more rewarding. Revision that relies solely on old notes and essays will put you off revising in general, and as a result you will revise less and do worse in your exams.

It is important to do *both* 'vision' (reading new books and having fresh ideas) *and* revision (relearning facts, arguments, and ideas, from lectures, seminars, notes and essays). Combine the two and alternate between them to avoid monotony. In general, try to keep yourself in an active rather than a passive frame of mind. You can do this when you are reading (as discussed in Chapter 5) and can also achieve it by rewriting old notes and essays and writing new practice essays (see below). Your goal is to make the arguments and information alive and active in your mind.

A revision plan

You will have a limited amount of time to revise for your exams. You should, at the start of the period you have available for revision, sit down and make a revision plan – a detailed timetable of the period available. Think about how many papers you have to revise for, which ones you need to spend slightly more time on, and so on. Then, perhaps dividing the day into three time slots of 3 hours each (such as 9–12, 2–5, 6–9), make a schedule that allocates an appropriate number of slots to each paper. You might decide that some days you would work all three slots, other days only two. You might also have to work around any paid work that you do. It is important not to be over-ambitious. Most people can't do productive intellectual work for more than about 6 hours in a day. Doing more than that will probably be counter-productive, increasing your levels of stress, anxiety and tiredness. Work all this out and make a schedule that allocates all your revision time to specific papers and tasks. This plan will make your revision much easier, more structured and more efficient. Below is a sample revision timetable for one week of a revision programme, for a history student preparing for exams on Tudor England, post-colonialism and the French Revolution. The student is particularly worried about the French Revolution paper and so has allocated that one the most sessions. On Tuesday and Friday evenings she has a part-time job.

	MON	TUES	WEDS	THURS	FRI
9–12	T.E. – look at lecture notes	F.R. – lecture notes	T.E. – primary sources	*COFFEE WITH EMILY*	T.E. – make essay plans
2–5	GYM	Library – new books on F.R.?	F.R. – primary sources	F.R. – primary sources	P-C – do practice exam paper
6–9	P-C – read essays	AT WORK	P-C – look for new stuff in library	F.R. – make essay plans	AT WORK

Healthy body, healthy mind

Some people, when it comes to revising for exams, lock themselves away all day and much of the night with their books and notes, cramming and studying intensively and unrelentingly for several weeks. Perhaps they do this because they have not been paying attention all year, or as a response to stress. It is not a healthy approach. They will end up drained, grey, tired, stressed and, probably, confused. Depriving themselves of sleep and exercise will have a particularly detrimental effect on their key mental powers of memory and analysis.

Your revision plan should allow plenty of time for fresh air, exercise, relaxation and sleep, if you want to be on top mental form in your exams. Going for a run (or a walk or a cycle ride or visiting the gym) can double up as both exercise and thinking time. But also make sure you have time off from thinking and find time to relax. (If your relaxation time sometimes involves a lot of alcohol, that is a less good idea, though. A lot of alcohol is very bad for your brain!)

Where to revise

When I was taking my finals as an undergraduate I often found that after an hour or two revising in one place I found it hard to carry on concentrating. One way to deal with this is to give yourself regular breaks (about 10 or 15 minutes per hour); another way is to vary the location of where you revise. There are plenty of different places that you might find congenial – in your room, in a café, in the park, in the library, in someone else's room, at your parents' house. Varying the location as well as the topic of revision quite regularly can help to stave off monotony.

Do practice papers

To be good at anything takes practice. Taking exams is no exception. Some people go into exams without having practised writing essays in exam conditions first. These people are badly prepared people.

In the weeks running up to your exams you should do at least one practice paper – preferably more – in exam conditions for each paper you're about to sit (for instance, you could do a previous year's exam paper, in a library, with no notes, allowing yourself the same amount of time as you will have in the exam itself). You could decide to do one or two timed essays per day during your revision period, and occasionally to do an entire practice paper. If you are very lucky, your lecturer might be prepared to mark a practice exam paper and give you feedback on ways to improve your performance for the real thing. In any case, doing practice papers is an essential part of exam preparation.

Some people avoid doing practice exams because it seems too daunting. But of course it is much better to get nerves and bad essays out of the way in practice exams that don't count for anything, than to wait for the real thing. If you have not done any practice exams before the real thing they will seem much more daunting than if you are already used to what it feels like to sit down with, say, 3 hours available to write three essays. It is particularly important to have a feel for how long you have available for each essay, how long you can reasonably spend writing an essay plan, and so on (see pages 159–60). There are few more stupid things you can do as an undergraduate sitting important exams that count towards your degree than to go in without having done some practice papers in exam conditions.

Question-spotting

Like doing practice papers, question-spotting is crucial preparation for taking an exam. Look at the exam papers that have been set over, say, the last 5 years. It will soon become clear that there are certain topics that come up very frequently; some may come up every single year.

Of course it might be that this year will be the first time in 5 years that a certain topic is left out of the exam, so past papers are not infallible guides. But they are very good guides. You should also be sure to ask your lecturers what will be in the exams. They will probably be happy to drop some fairly heavy hints. They want you to get good marks if at all possible, since that makes them look good, too.

If you have to write, say, three essays in the exam, it is probably a good idea to revise five topics on which questions come up very frequently or always. It is a very bad idea to go into the exam having prepared only for precisely the number of questions that you have to answer; if one or more of them fails to come up, you are in real trouble.

Understanding and memory

Like it or not, to do well in exams you have to use your memory. Some people are better at memorising things than others, but we are all capable of remembering a surprisingly large amount of information. This skill is one that is very useful to develop when taking exams.

However, before coming to this, the main point to take on board is that the key to being able to recall the right information in exams is not *memory* but *understanding*. If you have made the material your own by really thinking about it, understanding it, and developing your own line on it, you do not need any amazing feat of memory in order to be able to write about it in exam conditions. The less you understand of a topic, the more the task will seem to be one of committing alien material to memory. The more you understand it, the easier recall will be.

Even though understanding is the most important thing, there is also a place for actively committing certain things to memory. There are three sorts of thing that you can usefully commit to memory before sitting your exam paper: main themes for each topic, examples, and quotations.

Once you have picked the, say, five topics that you are going to revise for the exam, and you have done the appropriate amount of 'vision' and revision, a final step you could take is to produce a list of major themes that could be the main points you wanted to make in an exam essay. Such a list of themes for an essay on Darwinism and religion (see the analysis of the essay title in Chapter 4, page 53, and the sample introduction in Chapter 10, pages 142–3) might look like this:

Bible
Natural theology
Image of God?
Man's place in nature
New religion?

One trick you could try to help remember your major points is to take the first letter of each point (in this case B, N, I, M, N) and then make a memorable sentence using words starting with the same letters, such as 'By now I memorise nicely', or 'Belgian nomad is marrying Nora' or whatever. Then when you get into the exam, if there is a question similar to the one you prepared for on Darwin you will immediately think, say, 'By now I memorise nicely', and can then, hopefully, remember your list of main themes. If you do try to do something like this, it is important that you think of it as a checklist of important themes and points rather than as an essay 'plan' (for more on exam techniques, see 'Answer the question!' on pages 160–1).

You might also try to remember a particularly good example or two for each of your major points on a topic. Examples can be people, books, dates, events, and so on. Referring to names of individuals, the names of their books, the year in which a book was published, the year a significant event took place – all of these things are impressive if not essential. They are the sort of thing that can differentiate an essay with first-class content from an essay with adequate content.

Finally, for the real memory wizards, you might try to memorise a few particularly good quotations for each topic. Good quotations, as noted above, might be particularly well-expressed ideas, or memorable or famous phrases from important primary or secondary texts that you have read for the paper. You may find it useful to condense each topic you are revising on to a single 'crib sheet': a single page of notes that lists the key points, themes, dates, arguments, examples, or quotations that you need to commit to memory.

Taking exams

When you have revised from all your old notes, done some new reading, condensed each topic onto a single crib sheet and memorised all that you can, the day will come when it's time to take the exams. The day before, eat healthy food, take a walk, drink plenty of water and get a good night's sleep. On the day, have a final look at your notes and crib sheets. Then leave yourself plenty of time to get to the exam itself.

Read the instructions

Exams are quite stressful occasions and stress makes people behave in odd ways. This includes failing to do obvious things like reading the instructions at the top of the exam paper and following those instructions. A surprisingly large proportion of people have at one time or another failed to read the instructions on an exam paper or have failed to follow them and thus severely reduced their chances of success. Don't be one of those people! The very first thing you should do is to read every word on the exam paper carefully and be clear what is being asked of you – how many questions to answer, and from which sections of the paper, and so on. Don't assume that you know the instructions for the paper already – they might have changed this year, or you might have been misinformed.

Look at both sides of the sheet

Another very obvious point – look at both sides of the exam paper (or both sides of each sheet if there is more than one sheet). Make absolutely sure that you have looked at the whole paper and have not missed a couple of extra questions or a whole new section over the page.

Timing

It is essential that you divide your time evenly between each of your essays during the exam. You will seriously damage your chances of success if one of your essays is exceedingly short, scrappy, or non-existent. You should divide the total time available by the total number of essays you need to write. So, for example, if you have 3 hours to write four essays then you have 45 minutes per essay. Get a scrap of paper and write on it the time you need to start each new essay: '3.00 Essay 1, 3:45 Essay 2, 4:30 Essay 3, 5:15 Essay 4'. Stick to these times rigidly – even taking 5 or 10 minutes too long for each of the first three essays would leave you with nowhere near enough time for your final essay. Always be aware of how long you have had and how much time you have left for each essay.

Before writing each essay, allow a few minutes for *thinking* and for preparing a rough plan. This is essential if you are going to produce an interesting and relevant essay. If you have memorised a list of main themes for a topic, or some dates and examples, or quotations, then now is the time to scribble them all down on paper. Have a minute or two doing this, brainstorming, thinking of all the important points you need to mention in your answer (whether you have deliberately memorised any or not). Then draw up a very simple plan with just a word or two for each main paragraph. Make sure that your planned essay is going to answer the question that has been set, and be clear in your mind what your answer is and what sort of conclusion you are working towards. You should also include a rudimentary map at the start of your essay to help the examiners find their way through your answer more easily. The lack of time in an exam situation means that the map will be less detailed than it would be for a longer assessed essay, but it should still be there. Essays in which examiners get lost and disoriented get lower marks than easily navigable essays.

Also allow a few minutes at the end of each essay for reading it through to eliminate slips and blunders (spelling, grammar, missing words, and the like). The fact that you are writing under pressure of time makes it more likely that you will make mistakes and therefore more important to go back and check.

Answer the question!

Memorising lists of major points for each topic is probably a good idea. However, it is a very *bad* idea simply to find the title that roughly corresponds to your topic, write it at the top of your page, and then disgorge a prepared planned essay. Even though spotting likely topics is pretty easy, it is impossible to predict what actual question on the topic will come up. It is not that likely that a 'plan' you memorise for a topic will fit exactly the question that comes up. *Do not just reproduce a prepared essay if it does not fit the question!* Always answer the question. If your prepared list of themes and points on a topic doesn't really fit the question, there is no need to despair or panic, just spend a few minutes thinking about how to *tailor* the knowledge and understanding you have, and how to rearrange your points (which ones to discard, what new material to bring in) so as to answer the actual question that has been set. It is better to write an essay that really answers the question that might be, say, a little short on examples, than to write a well-prepared essay with lots of examples that answers a totally different question. Few things infuriate lecturers more than obviously pre-prepared essays that do not answer the question. (An essay that is simply a regurgitated version of a lecture you gave yourself is perhaps one of the few more infuriating things – see below.) Don't infuriate your lecturers!

One way to make it really clear you are answering the question is to use, in the course of your essay, the words and phrases used by the examiner in the essay title itself (see Chapter 10, pages 126–7).

Information, not waffle

Some exam questions are very general, abstract, or purely philosophical and do not explicitly ask for facts, dates, quotations, or references to primary and secondary material – for instance 'Would a world based on chance be incompatible with a purposeful God?' or 'Was Mozart a "great" composer?' or 'Is democracy an important component of international development?'. Do not be fooled! Do *not* give a vague, general, waffly answer. The examiners expect you to answer the question with reference to the knowledge you have acquired from your lectures, reading, seminars and essays. They expect you to show that you are familiar with the most important arguments on the topic, who made them, and in which books. They also expect you to be able to provide examples for any general points you make.

Some people think that referring to a primary or secondary text is a bad idea, since it shows that you are 'just' repeating what other people have said. But that is what you are *required* to do in an exam – that is precisely how you indicate that you have learned things during your course and have taken them on board. You will always get credit for referring to a primary or secondary text by name and showing that you know how one scholar differs from another in the way she approaches a problem. The only way that referring to primary or secondary texts could be anything other than a source of credit would be if it was *all* you did.

Analysis as well as information

As well as showing that you have learned the relevant facts and arguments, you are required in exam essays – as in coursework essays – to provide your own analysis. The essay should always be *driven* by your own argument; you also need to explain and analyse others' arguments.

The inside story – what examiners are *really* looking for

Having spent some years now setting and marking undergraduate exams, I have learned what it is like to be on the receiving end of exam scripts, and what examiners are really looking for. The following are the most important tips:

- *Don't be boring*! Marking exam scripts is, frankly, tedious. Reading essay after essay on the same subject can be mind-numbingly boring – all the more so if students simply regurgitate their lecture notes, and all the more so if it was a lecture you gave yourself! By far the best way to get in the examiner's good books, then, is to be *interesting*. Do not just regurgitate material from lectures and seminars. Show that you actually have a brain of your own and have thought about the question yourself. The need to do this is what makes it so essential to allow yourself some thinking time even in exam conditions. Make links with other topics and other areas of knowledge. Of course, you should not just be wacky for the sake of it. You will get a lower mark for being original and totally wrong than for being tedious. But do try to do the examiner a favour and brighten up his day by saying something interesting.
- *Communicate, don't regurgitate*. This is a similar point. Hopefully by the time you take your exams you will have made a lot of progress with developing your writing skills (see Chapter 10). Some people, when they get into exams, forget all about clarity of structure, language and argument, and leave their rhetorical and persuasive skills at home. For them, they are simply there to download tons of information onto the page. This is a mistake. In an exam essay as much as in an assessed essay or presentation you should think about your audience, how to keep them engaged with your argument, and how to persuade them to your point of view.
- *Provide evidence*. One of the big differences between first-class exam scripts and others is that the former back up their claims with evidence: quotations, dates, facts. Less good exam answers are full of generalisations, assertions and unsubstantiated opinions.

- *Write legibly.* There are few things more likely to lose you marks in an exam than messy or illegible handwriting. Examiners will not have the energy or inclination to try to decipher your writing if it is not easy to read. And they cannot give credit to anything that they cannot read.
- *Write with confidence.* Write in an assured way, indicating that you are confident both of your knowledge and of your interpretation. Do not feel that you have to hedge everything round with qualifications and exceptions. State your case and deploy your evidence clearly and boldly. Do not keep stating alternative points of view if they are not relevant. It is so much more pleasant to read a clear and confident essay than a cautious and indecisive one.
- *If possible, find out who is marking each exam you sit.* You should *not* then simply try to reproduce that lecturer's own views – that would make very boring reading (see 'Manage your teachers' in Chapter 2, pages 29–30). But you will at least have an idea of the sorts of question the lecturer thinks are interesting, the sorts of ways of thinking and writing that the lecturer likes, and also the questions and ideas that the lecturer thinks are worthless. This is useful information that you can use to your advantage.

Chapter 12

How to get a first

Summary

There is no set formula for getting a first. But if you make efficient use of your time, and understand the rules of the game – in other words, if you follow the advice in this book – you will increase your chances significantly. What you need to do to get a first can be summarised under two headings: executional excellence and innovation.

The secret of success

Sadly, there is no simple way to guarantee getting a first in your degree. But what I have tried to get across in this book is that there are some quite straightforward rules of the academic game that you can learn to play by in order to increase your chances. There are better and worse ways of using your time. Hopefully, after reading this book, you will feel better equipped to decide how best to spend your time on the particular course of study on which you are currently, or are about to become, engaged.

I said at the outset that I hoped this book would provide you with, amongst other things, a demystified idea of what constitutes first-class work. Perhaps I should take the opportunity of this final chapter to re-emphasise an obvious but important point: what I have been talking about in this book is what characterises first-class student *work*, not what characterises first-class *students* or first-class *people*. Whether or not you succeed in getting a first in the end is not a fundamental judgement about you as a person. Many highly intelligent and successful people do not get firsts (or do not even go to university). Do not identify yourself too closely with the academic work you produce. It is not a fundamental component of who you are, it is merely one of the many things that you do.

I hope that much of what I have said in the first 11 chapters has already contributed to giving you a clear idea of what constitutes first-class work. However, I have also included this brief final chapter to provide an explicit statement of *how to get a first*. I will start with a brief summary of the main points I have made so far, and then offer a further analysis of what this all really boils down to. First of all, then, the checklist of the main points in this book. What do you need to do to maximise your chances of getting a first?

✓ Understand the structure of your degree.
✓ Identify modes of assessment.
✓ Identify available resources.
✓ Become an expert user of libraries and the internet.
✓ Manage your time.
✓ Manage your teachers.
✓ Understand the difference between primary and secondary material.
✓ Identify and master the most important primary sources.
✓ Develop a strong voice of your own; have your own 'line'.
✓ Listen actively in lectures.
✓ Use seminars and classes to experiment with your ideas.
✓ Read and take notes actively and selectively.
✓ Make use of journal articles and books that are not on your reading list.
✓ Leave time for thinking before you start writing.
✓ Produce an argument; not a book report or a shopping list.
✓ Pay close attention to the title of your essay or presentation.
✓ Remember that a presentation is a performance.
✓ Make distinctions; do not rest content with vague generalisations.
✓ Grab your listeners' or readers' attention with an arresting first paragraph.
✓ Identify the scholarly debate to which you are contributing.
✓ Choose your words carefully.
✓ Write in plain English.
✓ Master the scholarly apparatus of footnotes and bibliographies.
✓ Read new material when revising.
✓ Keep healthy and well rested when revising.

✓   In exams, remember you are trying to interest and persuade your reader.
✓   Even in exams you need to give examples and evidence.
✓   Don't be boring!
✓   What is rewarded above all in academic work is the ability to argue your own case with confidence and clarity – in other words, being able to persuade your reader of your point of view using your own words and carefully selected evidence.

What this all boils down to is saying that there are two main elements to success at the highest level at university: *executional excellence* and *innovation*. The following applies to all assessed pieces of work: presentations, essays and dissertations.

Executional excellence

Executional excellence involves doing all the basics flawlessly.

An excellently executed piece of work contains no spelling, punctuation, grammatical or factual errors. As noted above, to be realistic, we all occasionally make such slips, but they should be kept to an absolute minimum. An excellently executed piece of work contains no ill-chosen, clumsy or unclear words, phrases, or sentences. An excellently executed piece of work is lucidly and logically structured and signposted, and is composed of clearly expressed, well-understood and persuasive arguments illustrated with powerful examples. An excellently executed piece of work displays a thorough understanding of the material covered in lectures and in set readings, perhaps including a few direct quotations from particularly important authors. An excellently executed piece of work answers the question that has been set.

An excellently executed piece of work might or might not be awarded a first (depending on how much evidence of interesting and creative thought it contains).

Innovation

Innovation involves making original, unexpected, and interesting points.

An innovative piece of work might take a counter-intuitive or unusual line of argument and make it seem reasonable and persuasive. An innovative piece of work might use an analogy with an entirely different topic, idea, or academic problem in order to shed new light on the question at hand. An innovative piece of work might make connections with knowledge and ideas learned in the context of a different subject to supplement material taken directly from lectures and readings, in order to create an interesting and original answer. An innovative piece of work might question the very assumptions upon which the question being asked is based, or it might argue strongly against the accepted line put forward in lectures or mainstream books on the subject.

An innovative piece of work might or might not be awarded a first (depending on whether the originality is intelligent and insightful or not, and on how well executed the piece of work is).

How to get a first

Excellently executed work that innovates in an intelligent way will certainly get a first. Good luck, and enjoy your studies!

Further reading

How to Get a First is a concise introductory guide to the skills you need in order to excel at university. I hope that through the course of your university career you will continue to reflect on how to read, think, argue and write more clearly and effectively. You will then want to consult more detailed and advanced books to accompany this further reflection. The best places to start are the other titles in the Routledge Study Guides series:

Robert Barrass, *Study!*, 2nd edn (London: Routledge, 2002).
Robert Barrass, *Students Must Write: A Guide to Better Writing in Coursework and Examinations*, 2nd edn (London: Routledge, 1995).
George Bernard, *Studying at University* (London: Routledge, 2003).
Geoffrey Squires, *Managing Your Learning* (London: Routledge, 2002).

The 'Speak-Write' series of books edited by Professor Rebecca Stott is also particularly helpful:

Rebecca Stott and Peter Chapman (eds), *Grammar and Writing* (Harlow: Longman, 2001).
Rebecca Stott, Anna Snaith and Rick Rylance (eds), *Making Your Case: A Practical Guide to Essay Writing* (Harlow: Longman, 2001).
Rebecca Stott, Tory Young and Cordelia Bryan (eds), *Speaking Your Mind: Oral Presentation and Seminar Skills* (Harlow: Longman, 2001).
Rebecca Stott and Simon Avery (eds), *Writing with Style* (Harlow: Longman, 2001).

On time management and other good mental habits, I strongly recommend:

Gillian Butler and Tony Hope, *Manage Your Mind: The Mental Fitness Guide* (Oxford: Oxford University Press, 1995).

On the use of evidence (of interest and relevance to more than just historians):

E. H. Carr, *What Is History?*, new edn (Basingstoke: Palgrave, 2001).
John Vincent, *An Intelligent Person's Guide to History* (London: Duckworth, 1996).

On public speaking skills:

Dominic Hughes and Benedict Phillips, *The Oxford Union Guide to Successful Public Speaking* (London: Virgin, 2000).

A couple of informative and diverting books on referencing and punctuation:

Anthony Grafton, *The Footnote: A Curious History* (London: Faber and Faber, 1997).
Lynne Truss, *Eats, Shoots & Leaves: The Zero Tolerance Approach to Punctuation* (London: Profile Books, 2003).

And finally, three new editions of classic guides to good writing:

Henry Fowler, *Fowler's Modern English Usage*, new edn (Oxford: Oxford University Press, 2002).
Eric Partridge, *Usage and Abusage: A Guide to Good English*, 3rd edn (London: Penguin, 1999).
William Strunk Jr, with E. B. White, *The Elements of Style*, 4th edn (Boston, MA and London: Allyn and Bacon, 2000).

Index

adverbs: overuse of 138
analysis and synthesis 132–3
apostrophes 106–7
articles *see* journals and journal
  articles
assessment *see* degree courses; essays

bibliography 7, 47–51, 63–5, 80–2,
  123; *see also* libraries, reading
  lists
books 42–3; using contents and
  index 46–7, 54–6; *see also*
  reading

Cambridge *see* Oxford and
  Cambridge
classes *see* seminars
COPAC *see* internet
courses *see* degree courses
coursework *see* essays

degree courses: combined honours
  22; methods of assessment 22–4;
  structure of 21–3
dictionary definitions 128–9
dissertations 23, 150–1

e.g. 70, 109
employment after graduation 13–15
'essayese' versus plain English
  135–40
essays: argument 88–91, 126–33;
  assessed coursework essays 6–7,
  22–4, 150–1; beginnings 142–7;

endings 147–8; essay-writing
  5–7, 125–51; numbered points
  in 130–1; planning 85–8, 91–2;
  structure 140–50; thinking about
  the title 53–4, 88, 126–7
evidence: use of 11–12, 133–5,
  169; collection of 65–6, 96–8
exams 22–4, 158–63; fear of
  152–3; *see also* revision
extra-curricular activities 13, 27–9

first person 10–11
footnotes *see* referencing

geniuses and non-geniuses 17–19
grammar and spelling: common
  mistakes corrected 105–19

handwriting 104–5
he, she or they 109–11
hyphens 111

i.e. 71, 109
indexes *see* books
internet: academic uses of 75;
  bibliographic uses 46–7, 80–2;
  COPAC 65, 80–1; finding
  background information 77–8;
  finding biographical information
  78–80; finding dates 76–7;
  JSTOR 81–2; online texts and
  journals 43, 81–3; PORTAL
  83–4
its and it's 106

journals and journal articles 24, 26, 43–6, 50–1, 81–2, 119, 123, 143–4, 151
JSTOR *see* internet

language: clarity of 135–40
laptops 62
Latin phrases and abbreviations 68–72
learning: active and passive 33–4
lectures 34–7; handouts 36; taking notes in 37–8
lecturers 8–9; as a resource to be managed 29–32, 34–5, 37–8; what they are really looking for 162–3
libraries and catalogues 14, 16, 24–6, 42–3, 47–51, 61–2, 65, 151, 153; COPAC 65, 80–1; *see also* internet; reading
literally 111–12

note-taking 61–8; *see also* lectures

online resources *see* internet
opinion and evidence 10–12, 30; *see also* evidence
oral exams *see* presentations
Oxford and Cambridge 7, 17, 31

paragraphs as building blocks 141–2
passive and active voices 137
plagiarism 62, 135
plain English *see* 'essayese' versus plain English
planning *see* essays; presentations
PORTAL *see* internet
presentations: delivery 100–3, 169; fear of 94–5; as performance 95; planning 98–100; researching 96–8; visual aids 96–7
primary and secondary material 24–7, 39–40, 59–61, 65

pronouns 109–11, 114–15
punctuation 107–9, 111, 169

quotations 65, 115, 133–5

reading: actively 51–4, 59–61, 66–7; around the subject 47–51; *see also* reading lists; skim-reading
reading lists 43–51
referencing 7, 119–22; *see also* bibliography
researching *see* evidence; libraries and catalogues; reading; reading lists
revision 153–8; memorising material 157–8; new material 153–4; practice papers 156; question-spotting 156–7; revision plan 154–5

school and university: differences 7–11
seminars 38–41
sentences: conjunction at start of 10, 106; and non-sentences 115–17; preposition at end of 113; short and long 148–50
skim-reading 56–8
spelling *see* grammar and spelling
split infinitives 117
supervisions *see* lecturers
synonyms: overuse of 10, 136

teachers *see* lecturers; school and university
tenses 117
that and which 118
their and they're 118–19
time-management 27–9, 51–3, 154–5, 168
transferable skills 13–15
tutorial time *see* lecturers